Called to Care

Resources by Palmer Becker

Called to Care: A Training Manual for Small Group Leaders
Called to Equip: A Training and Resource Manual for Pastors
Called to Lead Video, based on *Called to Care*
and *Called to Equip*
Creative Family Worship
(To order the above, please call 1-800-759-4447.)

Called to Care Study Guide
Called to Care Audio Seminar
(To order the above, please contact the author by e-mail,
palmer@southwind.net; or by phone, 1-316-327-4221.)

Called to Care

*A Training Manual
for Small Group Leaders*

Palmer Becker

HERALD PRESS
Scottdale, Pennsylvania
Waterloo, Ontario

Library of Congress Cataloging-in-Publication Data
Becker, Palmer, 1936-
   Called to care : a training manual for small group leaders / Palmer
Becker.
      p.   cm.
   Includes bibliographical references.
   ISBN 0-8361-3622-5 (alk. paper)
   1. Church group work. 2. Small groups. 3. Lay ministry. I. Title.
BV652.2.B427   1993
253'.7—dc20   93-12086

Unless otherwise indicated, Scripture quotations are taken from the
Holy Bible, New International Version®. Copyright © 1973, 1978, 1984
International Bible Society. Used by permission of Zondervan Bible
Publishers. All rights reserved.

CALLED TO CARE
Copyright © 1993 by Herald Press, Scottdale, Pa. 15683
   Published simultaneously in Canada by Herald Press,
   Waterloo, Ont. N2L 6H7. All rights reserved
Library of Congress Catalog Card Number: 93-12086
International Standard Book Number: 0-8361-3622-5
Printed in the United States of America
Book design by Gwen M. Stamm/Cover art by Joel Kauffmann
05 04 03 02 01 00   10 9 8 7 6 5 4

To order or request information, please call
1-800-759-4447 (individuals); 1-800-245-7894 (trade).
Website: www.mph.org

To a new generation of lay pastors

Contents

Acknowledgments 10

PART I   THE VISION

Introduction 13

1 A Caring Congregation 16

Observe needs, be committed to caring, ground your vision in
Scripture, clarify basic assumptions, get the big picture, and
be part of the team

PART II   TYPES OF GROUPS

2 The Nurture Group 27

Understand its purpose, decide what ministry means for you,
recruit your group, begin with a cup of coffee and a covenant,
meet in homes with a timed agenda, choose a curriculum,
and celebrate a good conclusion

3 The Support Group 36

Identify people in need of special support, offer an empathic
listening ear, gather the group, agree to a covenant, and
begin with the felt need

4 The Evangelistic Group **42**

Get excited about evangelism, plan your strategy, invite your friends, be clear but flexible, plan your meeting, take the lead in showing acceptance, and share your faith

5 The Mission Group **52**

Be committed to do Christ's work, sound a call, clarify the basics, hold the call and discern the gifts, attend to both inward and outward agendas, discover the resources needed, and conclude with honor

PART III   BASIC ELEMENTS

6 Acceptance **63**

Accept each member, share your life histories, ask a sharing question, listen actively, respond reflectively, use food as a tool, and listen as people leave

7 Bible Study **72**

Believe in Bible study, have a clear aim, research the background, begin with an interesting introduction, ask three main questions, and clinch the main point

8 Prayer **81**

Respond to God, clarify basic ground rules, help new people begin, converse with God, use a variety of patterns, organize a prayer chain, and expand prayer to worship

9 Mission **88**

Be committed to mission, support members in ministry, choose a group project, and choose to grow

PART IV   LEADERSHIP ISSUES

10 Leadership **95**

Don't manipulate or force your way, seek the needed qualities, accept the responsibility, choose your leadership style and pattern, and lead a dialogue

11 Group Participation 103

Get all members involved, discuss through dialogue, learn to model and lead dialogue, continue to increase participation, discern the gifts and roles, and keep an open climate

12 Creativity and Conflict 111

Encourage creativity, recognize that conflict is inevitable, identify the sources of conflict, deal with the conflict immediately, follow tested mediation steps, and face other problems with courage

13 Supervision and Continuing Education 120

Welcome regular supervision, work closely with your pastor, meet monthly with your peers, welcome continuing education, and keep your purpose clear

Appendixes 126

A. Group Member Ministry Report
B. Care Group Record Sheet
C. Monthly Leaders Check-in Sheet
D. In-depth Ministry Assessment Form
E. Focus Questions
F. Possible Themes for Continuing Education
G. Training Program Evaluation Form

Notes 135
The Author 138

Acknowledgments

I am indebted to a number of persons for sparking within me and my wife, Ardys, a vision for small groups. Among these are Gordon Cosby, pastor of the Church of the Saviour; Lyman Coleman, director of Serendipity House; Roberta Hestenes, president of Eastern Baptist Seminary; and Carl F. George of the Fuller Institute. I am deeply grateful for their work, from which I have drawn heavily.

I am also thankful for Leonard Wiebe, who led a workshop on small groups in the first church I served in Clinton, Oklahoma; for Ed Goertzen, whom I watched as he effectively coordinated nearly fifty groups in the Willingdon Mennonite Brethren Church, Burnaby, B.C., and who helped as we set up and maintained a Care Group ministry at Peace Mennonite Church, Richmond, B.C.; and for our son, Byron, who participated in and interpreted small group life at Assembly Mennonite Church, Goshen, Indiana.

This book is dedicated to small group leaders everywhere. They in effect are a new generation of pastors. Through small groups we can be God's caring people in new and more effective ways.

—*Palmer Becker*
Hesston, Kansas

PART I The Vision

Introduction

For nearly two thousand years Christians have been meeting together in small groups. Jesus brought together a small group of twelve men. The early Christians broke bread in their homes and ate together with glad and sincere hearts. The Anabaptist, Methodist, and Pentecostal movements began in small groups.

Christians today are again taking a new interest in small groups. In groups of five to twelve, people are finding new opportunities to grow spiritually. They are finding a new quality of fellowship as they share and pray together. Wherever renewal or growth is happening, small groups are involved.

People like what they see in small groups. The early church enjoyed the favor of all the people and the Lord added daily those who were being saved (Acts 2:47). Why?

Deep, caring, accountable, relationships bring a new quality to a family of Christian brothers and sisters. The Bible refers to such a family as the bride of Christ. To find such a family is to find a pearl of great price. It is a treasure for which people are willing to give up much or all.

The early church grew from a handful to three thousand, to

five thousand, and more, in a very short time. The Anabaptist movement grew in two years from a small group to two thousand, in a decade to twelve thousand, and in a century to 160 thousand. The Methodist groups of ten begun by John Wesley in the 1700s attracted thousands until they became a denomination of 12 million. Christians under persecution in China during this century had a deep care for each other in house groups. People liked what they saw, joined them, and as a result, the church grew from 4 million to 15, or perhaps even 30 million in forty years.

What is your vision for the church? What should the church be? How do you propose that we get there? No one can give a vision to another person. Each of us needs to capture the vision that God has for us.

Called to Care proposes that God wants us to be a caring people and that small groups are the best vehicle for helping us get there. "In no other situation can the functions of the church be so fully carried out," says John Mallison. "In no other context can the word of God be communicated with so much impact on lives. The church today, as the church of the New Testament, needs the church in the house." [1]

Called to Care has a vision for congregations who are moving beyond teaching and learning to a focus on caring and reconciliation. This manual encourages ministry by the laity. It recognizes that small group leaders can function as lay pastors to a small group of people in the church. Carl F. George of the Fuller Institute is convinced that if properly led and supervised by their pastor, small group leaders will take ministry to their small group so seriously they will prefer such ministry to the recognition of elected office. [2]

Small groups, called Care Groups in this manual, are person-centered. They care about people. They begin where people are in their understanding of the Bible, prayer, and the Christian faith. As a Care Group leader, you will be trained to begin by listening for the loneliness, distress, and special needs in peoples lives.

With the use of eighty imperative statements, *Called to Care* will help you through step-by-step exploration of a vision for groups. You will examine various types of groups, then investigate what it takes to begin and lead a group. You will be introduced to such skills as active listening, reflective dialogue, leading Bible study, defining mission, and leading in prayer.

You will not be alone in this experience. It is suggested that other potential Care Group leaders and an apprentice be recruited to study and learn with you. Your pastor or overall coordinator will lead you in a model Care Group experience and use this manual to explore basic small group principles. In the process, you will learn to know your pastor or overall coordinator in a new and closer way. After your group begins, supportive supervision and continuing education will be offered.

It is recommended that the training be done over a thirteen-week period of time. Each week you will study one unit from a Bible study guide plus one chapter from this manual. At the end of each chapter, you will find an evaluation exercise which you will be asked to complete. It will help you to evaluate the group meeting that you have just experienced and to learn the basic principle of the chapter. An alternate training model is to have a weekend or one-day training retreat in which just one Bible study is modeled together with a study of the material in this manual.

A companion manual, *Called to Equip,* is a resource and training guide for pastors. It furnishes the helps needed to set up and maintain a Care Group ministry in your church. In it your pastor will find resources to enable you to lead a group with sensitivity and competence.

These materials are offered to you with a prayer that God will use Care Groups to open a new chapter in your life and your church as they have in ours.

1 A Caring Congregation

Observe the Needs

People go to where their needs are met. They go to school when they need learning or to work when they need income. They go home at the end of the day for food and rest. More and more people around the world are going to small groups to satisfy their needs for deeper relationships, a more meaningful spiritual life, and emotional support.

We live in a time and world characterized by individualism and isolation. Natural networks of supportive relationships like family, workplace, and neighborhood are breaking down. Children have their own rooms at home and workers their own equipment at work. The closer people live to each other as neighbors, the higher they build the walls.

The competitiveness, dishonesty, and temptations of our age are pulling us apart from each other and God. We have become a society of individuals who are independent, lonely, and insecure. People on the outside may look like they have it all together but on the inside they are hurting. People need healthy relationships!

Supportive relationships cause us to grow. People are looking for more than health and wealth. They are looking for a climate of acceptance, genuineness, and empathy. Deep down they are seeking the sense of community available in a caring congregation broken down into caring groups.

Along with this need for a caring community is a new quest for spirituality. Many isolated individuals and families have been reaching out to social workers, the human potential movement, the New Age movement, and a variety of secular programs to meet spiritual and social needs. A caring group and a caring congregation can do much to meet these needs.

The church ought to be the one place in this world where life-giving, caring relationships are developed. That is the purpose of the church! But too often the church is one more impersonal, fragmented institution that does not listen or care.

Be Committed to Caring

Care Groups make a difference! They can help your church become what it is meant to be. In dialogue with each other, caring people can develop committed and trusting relationships with God and with other people. You will find that caring people who listen are appreciated. People committed to care have the qualities possessed by the early church, which enjoyed "the favor of all the people" and as a result, "the Lord added to their number daily those who were being saved" (Acts 2:47).

When we provide the therapeutic climate, God can make that kind of Spirit happen again. Kenneth C. Haugk says it well, "We need to do the caring. God will do the curing."[3]

Paul Tournier, noted Swiss psychiatrist says, "Ninety percent of peoples problems are best dealt with by fellow strugglers, not psychiatrists, doctors, or clergy." [4] Chuck Colson of Prison Ministries Fellowship says, "No Christian can grow strong and stand the pressures of this life unless he is surrounded by a small group of people who minister to him and build him up in the faith." [5]

God's purpose in sending his Son was to provide a way to bring all things together in him (Eph. 1). The church is to be God's agent of love and reconciliation in this world. The church's primary goal is to bring people into fellowship with each other and the Lord. Such relationships help people to be and to do what God envisions for them.

A Care Group is like the twelve disciples, or like a family—a spiritual family brought into being by a loving Father. Jesus envisioned the brothers and sisters who make up this family comforting each other. They would teach each other, remind each other of the truth, then help each other act according to God's will.

The good news is that when people come together in a Christ-centered, caring fellowship, they have the best potential for becoming what they were intended to be—a sharing, forgiving, serving community of people who meet each others' needs and reach out in love to the world.

Ground Your Vision in Scripture

Throughout biblical history God has used both large and small groups to do his work. In the wilderness God used Moses to minister to the whole congregation of Israel but through Jethro advised that the people meet in ministry groups of ten (Exod. 18:10-27). Jesus spoke to the five thousand but spent more time with his group of twelve than with all the rest of the people put together. In the early church, large groups of new Christians met in the temple for general instruction but then met in homes for more personal sharing (Acts 2:46).

God calls his people into covenant relationships so that they can function well in the world. Being in meaningful relationship with God and fellow believers is not optional for a Christian. That is the essence of the church!

Small groups are essential because of the *quality of life* God wants us to have. Jesus said, "By this all men will know that you are my disciples, if you love one another" (John 13:35). If we are truly to love one another, we must get to know each other at a deeper level than our larger congregational settings allow. Face-to-face groups make that possible.

Small groups provide the *context for salvation*. We are not saved in an isolated, individualistic way. We experience the forgiveness, acceptance, and power of Christ in the context of his community. Jesus talks about being born again into a new family of brothers and sisters (John 1:12; 3:3-8; Luke 8:19-21).

Care Groups are the *context for spiritual growth*. God wants us to be made into Christ's image by the transforming of our minds (Rom 12:2). Interaction and dialogue in caring groups calls us to accountability—which helps us become Christlike in our minds and actions.

Care Groups also equip us for *witness and service*. In small groups we discern each others' gifts and help each other use them for the common good. Small groups are an excellent setting "to prepare God's people for works of service" (Eph. 4:12).

Clarify Basic Assumptions

Basic assumptions can help us talk the same language and visualize the same outcomes. Following are five basic assumptions that undergird the Care Group ministry outlined in this manual.

1. Our God who lives in community wants each of us to also experience the richness and support of community.

2. The church is to be God's caring community. A caring community becomes most concrete in small groups of twelve or less.

3. Lay persons (both male and female) can take responsibility for a small group of people and invest the time and energy needed to learn the skills required for competent ministry.

4. Pastors of caring congregations will encourage ministry by the laity and will shift time to recruit, train, commission, and supervise them to excellence.

5. Caring groups which meet in homes have unique healing and evangelistic powers. They have the potential for being both the key pastoral and the primary evangelistic structure of the church.

Get the Big Picture

A caring church needs preaching and worship services to inspire people toward commitment. Teaching and study classes are needed to learn the content of Scripture and of the Christian faith. A missing element in many churches is dialogue. Dialogue should always remain the primary form of communication in a Care Group. Small groups should be characterized by careful listening and reflective response.

Pastors of caring churches will lead teams of Care Group leaders who do pastoral work. Rather than doing all the ministry themselves, pastors will see to it that the ministry is done. Their responsibility is to be leaders of leaders. In this way pastors' effectiveness can be multiplied and they can be spared burnout. Pastors will recruit and train Care Group leaders, then meet with this team of leaders at least once a month to offer up to two hours of supportive supervision and continuing education. The leadership team might be diagramed as follows.

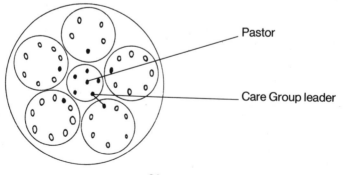

Pastor

Care Group leader

Care Group leaders seek to mobilize all congregational members for ministry. A bell curve of a local congregation indicates that generally about 10 percent of attenders are deeply involved, 80 percent mildly involved, and 10 percent uninvolved. Instead of activating the potential 80 percent force, leaders often do most of the work themselves. Care Group leaders aim to make the uninvolved doers of the Word and not hearers only (Jas. 1:22).

The bell curve can be depicted as follows.[6]

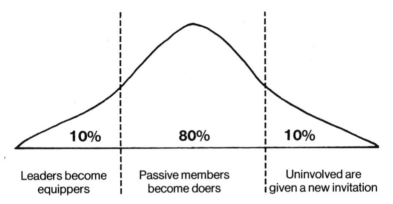

10%	80%	10%
Leaders become equippers	Passive members become doers	Uninvolved are given a new invitation

Most Care Groups will have between five and twelve members. People will come together in groups around common interests or needs. They will meet regularly—whether weekly, biweekly, or monthly—usually in someone's home. What is shared in the group will be kept confidential. Members will care for each other, pray for each other, and help each other in times of need. Most groups will be open and will actively seek others who might want to join them.

Training, followed by an interview, will be offered to potential Care Group leaders. The pastor will recommend approval of Care Group leaders to the church council/board. Persons affirmed by the council will be commissioned for ministry. Care Group leaders together with their apprentices will recruit people for groups or lead groups that form in other ways. Their ministry will be seen equal in importance to any ministry in the church and will be safeguarded at all costs.

Be Part of the Team

This manual is a call to action inviting you to become the leader of a Care Group. You are invited to explore the possibility of seeing small groups as the basic pastoral structure of the church. The invitation is to caring relationships that will change peoples lives and bring new people into the church.

The church is where we study the Bible together to see what it means for our lives. The church is where we pray personally for each other. The church is where we function as a caring family of brothers and sisters. We fulfill all these functions best in small groups of twelve or less. Perhaps a church should never have more than twelve members! A healthy congregation needs to be a congregation of groups working in close harmony with each other. You are invited to be part of the team that leads such a congregation of groups.

Basic Assumptions
An Exercise

Each Care Group meeting in this training series will end with a time of teaching, evaluation, and feedback to help apply the basic point of the chapter. We begin this series of studies with an evaluation of basic assumptions. On the following Lichert scales, indicate how strongly you disagree or agree with the definitions, basic assumptions, and statements given.

	Strongly Disagree			Strongly Agree	
	1	2	3	4	5
1. Deep down most people in our congregation and community are looking for a sense of community.	1	2	3	4	5
2.There is a new quest for spirituality in our church and community.	1	2	3	4	5
3. All too often our church is perceived as an impersonal, fragmented institution that does not listen or care.	1	2	3	4	5
4. Our God who lives in community wants each of us also to experience the richness and support of community.	1	2	3	4	5
5. The church is to be a caring community. This caring community becomes most concrete in small groups of twelve or less.	1	2	3	4	5
6. Lay persons both male and female are able to take responsibility for a small group of people and will invest the time and energy required to learn the skills required.	1	2	3	4	5
7. Our pastor will encourage ministry by the laity and will shift time to recruit, train, commission, and supervise lay persons to excellence.	1	2	3	4	5
8. Caring groups which meet in homes have unique healing and evangelistic powers. They have the potential for being both the key pastoral and the evangelistic structure of our church.	1	2	3	4	5

PART II Types of Groups

A small group is an intentional, face-to-face gathering of three to twelve people meeting on a regular basis with a common purpose. A small group is informal. It is an organism, not an organization. A small group is a cell, not a class. It is person-centered rather than idea-centered. A small group is made up of honest, open, accepting people who get together regularly for dialogue on a subject of common interest.

A Christian small group is a miniature church. It is the smallest unit of the worldwide church. It seeks to come as close as possible to being the kingdom of God on earth. Bruce Larson describes the kingdom of God as the kingdom of four right relationships—(1) a right relationship with God, (2) a right relationship with one's self, (3) a right relationship with others, and (4) a right relationship with the world.[7] Small groups seek to practice these relationships.

The next four chapters will describe four types of small groups. You will be invited to choose which type is right for you. The four are: nurture groups, support groups, evangelistic groups, and mission groups. The four are similar in that they are all small, somewhat informal, and interpersonal. They are all called "Care Groups" but each is somewhat different in terms of purpose, agenda, and content. Because each is different, each will attract a different kind of people, study different kinds of materials, and organize its agendas in different ways.

What is your most basic need or challenge? Who else might have that need? What type of group will best meet the need? With these questions in mind, read the next four chapters, then dialogue concerning what group is right for you.

2 The Nurture Group

Understand Its Purpose

A nurture group is pastoral. It seeks to help those who are already Christians to care for each other and grow in faith. It aims to help each member of the group experience fellowship in place of loneliness, acceptance and support in place of alienation, and spiritual growth in place of stagnation.

In more and more congregations, Care Groups are becoming the key pastoral structure. Persons who want good pastoral care need to get into a group! Nurture groups are based on the belief that God has given lay people and lay leaders the gifts to minister to each others needs and to celebrate each other's joys. When a member of a Care Group becomes ill or has a need to talk, the other members, and possibly the leader of the group, will be the first persons available.

Three basic promises form the basis of a nurturing Care Group.

- We will meet together regularly to encourage each other in Christ.
- We will pray for each other by name and be available when another member is in need.

• We will refuse to speak or listen to a word of criticism behind the back of another member.

Decide What Ministry Means for You

As a Care Group leader, you will be part of the pastoral team of the church. You will minister to the small group of persons entrusted to you. Pray for each member. Get to know as much as you can about each person. Take the lead in encouraging that person in Christ!

Jesus told his first followers to teach new Christians to obey everything I have commanded you (Matt. 28:20.) The apostle Paul told Timothy, "The things you have heard me say in the presence of many witnesses entrust to reliable men who will also be qualified to teach others" (2 Tim. 2:2). To the Ephesians Paul gave clear instructions that pastors and teachers were not to do it all themselves. They were "to prepare [equip] all of God's people for works of service" (Eph. 4:11-12).

As New Testament Christians who believe in the ministry of all believers, we are to minister to each other and those we meet in daily life. John Maxwell of Skyline Methodist Church in San Diego says, "No ministry, no membership!" Your task as a leader is to help ministry happen. As you are taught in ministry, you in turn are to equip and encourage group members in their ministries.

Don't panic! Serving as a lay pastor to even a small group of people for a week may seem like an enormous responsibility. But your pastor or overall coordinator will provide you with skill training, encouragement, and backup when you need it. You will meet regularly with other Care Group "pastors" to explore how you can give the best care to your group members.

In discussions with your pastor, you will explore your particular ministry functions. These will likely include convening the group on a regular basis, usually once a week. You will likely serve as a facilitator of study, sharing, prayer, and perhaps worship. You are not to be superhuman. In fact, as a servant, you will want to learn and experience as much from your members as they do from you.

As a lay pastor, you may occasionally want to visit individually with each group member. You may do this in their home or place of work. Pay special attention to them on Sunday morning. If they are absent, tell them they were missed. Some churches ask their small group leaders to serve communion or to assist in the baptizing of new converts who have come to faith in the context of a group. (If you wish to explore further the concept of the small group leader as pastor of a group, read *20/20 Vision* by Dale Galloway[8] or *Can the Pastor Do it Alone?* by Melvin J. Steinbron.[9]) Your pastor will go over a job description with you.

Recruit Your Group

Pastoral or nurture groups generally form when three or more people feel a need to go deeper in their Christian life. These people find each other in various ways. They have affinity for each other.

Usually the best way to gather a group is by personal invitation. Find another person or couple who shares the same need or burden as you do. Talk about your need and how it might be met. Seek to answer the following questions.

- What is our need and purpose? Why do we want to meet?
- Who else might be interested in meeting with us?
- What will we study? What materials might we use?
- Who will lead and how? (Express your willingness.)
- Where and when should we gather to brainstorm?

As you draw up a list of other persons or couples who might be interested in meeting, do not make it too cozy. A variety of age, gender, and background perspectives will add interest to group life. Invite a person or two who are sitting on the edge. They will be your church growth people and may bring another dimension to the group.

Draft a clear purpose statement that you can use to invite the persons on your list to the first meeting. An example might be: "The purpose of our Care Group is to meet weekly to share our experiences, to study the Sermon on the Mount, and to pray for each other." Alternatives might be "to have a potluck meal once a month" or "to discuss a book of the month."

Before you begin inviting the persons you have listed to a first meeting, share your initial plans with your pastor—who may have additional insights, materials to consider, and helpful encouragement. Discuss whether or not you want the organizational meeting announced in the bulletin.

Choose a place, set a date, and invite the persons on your list on the basis of your stated purpose. You may do this by personal conversation, phone, or a letter to be confirmed by phone. Three or four is enough to start a group. Since not everyone may agree to be in the group, you may need to invite several more than you expect to come. Ask widely and personally. You may be surprised who has the same needs and vision! If too many come, help a second group form.

Even after your group is formed, draw an empty chair into the circle at the end of each meeting and ask the group to pray for someone to fill the chair at the next meeting. Be an open group. Be committed to minister to more people as you are being ministered to. When you reach nine persons in the group, divide into fours or fives for your Bible study or commission several members to begin a new group.

Begin with a Cup of Coffee and a Covenant

As you gather for your first meeting, begin with a cup of coffee and some refreshments. If some of the invitees are not acquainted, introduce them to each other. As you begin, ask a sharing question everyone can answer: "What do you do on a typical Wednesday?" or "Tell us where you were born and what your family was like when you were seven years old."

After this initial sharing, seek to clarify the interest in and possible purpose for a group. You might open the subject by saying, "If we would meet together regularly, what would be the purpose of our coming together?" Don't begin by giving the purpose you outlined in your invitation! Let the purpose and ownership of the group come back from the potential members.

Let different points of view be expressed. Very likely one person will inwardly disagree with the expressed purpose. Watch out for premature closure! All disagreements and alternate purposes for the group must be heard and discussed or they will later rise up to divide or destroy the group. As you reach consensus on your purpose, poll the group to be sure you are in touch with each person's thoughts and feelings and that all expectations are clear. If someone does not feel the group will be helpful, he or she can opt out.

After the purpose of the group is clear, agree on housekeeping details. Where will we meet? Is this the best time? What materials will be needed? What will it cost? Who will take responsibility for what? To assist you in reviewing the important points, and to be sure that you have come to consensus, ask someone to check if you have covered all the points in the Our Group Covenant form at the end of this chapter.

As your group concludes its discussion of the covenant, share your enthusiasm and desire to see the group succeed. Recognize that to succeed, group members must give priority to the group, be personally available to each other, and treat what is shared in the group as confidential. To confirm these agreements, you might ask four specific questions.

1. Can we agree to meet regularly once a week for the next eight weeks? If for some reason you need to be absent, can we agree that you will call the leader or the host in advance?

2. Can we agree to pray for each other regularly?

3. If one of us has a physical, emotional, or spiritual need, can we do our best to be available to help meet that need?

4. Can we agree that what is shared in this group will not be shared with anyone else unless permission has been received to do so?[10]

When you have reached agreement, take the Our Group Covenant form to your pastor and to the first monthly meeting of group leaders. Let them help you resolve any questions about materials or covenant.

Meet in Homes with a Timed Agenda

Nurture groups generally meet in homes. They should begin and end on time. Usually they do not run longer than ninety minutes. A typical evening might include:

Opening (30 Minutes)
- Greetings and introductions
- Refreshments
- A sharing question (see chapter 6)

Bible study (30 minutes)
- Introduction
- Dialogue questions
- Practical application

Sharing, planning, and prayer (30 minutes)
- Reports on mission projects and answers to prayer
- Sharing of personal concerns and prayer

After adjournment
- More coffee and informal conversation
- Personal follow-up and ministry as needed

Choose a Curriculum

There are many materials available for use by nurture Care

Groups. Generally you will want to do Bible study in your group, although for variety you might occasionally choose a book relevant to the needs of the group. Some Bible studies from which to choose include:

Faith and Life Bible Series[11]
Genesis 1–11
Genesis 12–50
Isaiah
1 Peter
Revelation (and others)

Serendipity House Materials[12]
Sermon on the Mount
Parables
Beginner Group Series (Get Acquainted)
Group Bible Study (No homework)
Mastering the Basics (With homework)

Judy Hamlin has brought together *A Curriculum and Small Group Resource Guide*[13] which lists and evaluates over 1,000 topical and Bible study resources. Many of these can be examined in a Christian bookstore.

If you choose a prepared study guide, let it be your servant, not your master. Don't feel obligated to use all of the questions. Consider them as suggestions. (See chapter 7 for help on preparing discussion questions in relationship to the aim you choose for a study.)

Celebrate a Good Conclusion

Think of your group as an ongoing group. But initially give the group freedom to think in terms of one unit at a time. When the group comes to the end of its first cycle, usually eight to twelve weeks, invite the group to recovenant. By then the group may have moved from being dependent on you as leader to independence or some level of interdependence. (Chapter 12 will discuss these stages in group life.)

Recovenanting calls for a new look at your purpose and a continuing or growing commitment to each other. It invites you to examine the disciplines needed for fulfilling your purpose. If the original purpose for the group has been met, the group needs to conclude its existence as a group or formulate a new purpose.

At least annually, each group in the church should fill out a Group Covenant form, take it to the pastor or group leaders meeting, and give a reason for the group's existence. Groups that do not have a clear purpose or that have not added new people will usually die out in eighteen months to two years.

If your group has fulfilled or lost its purpose, bring the group to a clear and deliberate conclusion. This is better than letting members become irregular and then feeling guilty for having caused the group to fail. Help the group members share the benefits they have received from being in the group and to celebrate a good conclusion.

For a further study of nurture groups and resources for them, you might want to read *Good Things Come in Small Groups* written by a small group (Downers Grove, Ill.: Inter-Varsity Press, 1985) and *Covenant to Care* by Louis H. Evans, Jr., (Wheaton, Ill.: Victor Books, 1982).

Our Group Covenant

An Application Exercise[14]

1. The purpose of our group is. . . . (check one or more)
   ____to care for each other.
   ____to know God's will more clearly through Bible study.
   ____to support each other in our struggles and ministries.
   ____to reach out to others.
   ____other

2. We will study. . . .

3. The main version of the Bible to be used will be. . . .

4. Our leader will be. . . .

5. His/her responsibilities will be to. . . .

6. We will meet regularly:
   on _____ (day of week or month).
   from _____ to _____ (beginning and closing times).
   at _____(place or places).
   for _____weeks, at which time we will review our group and
       future plans.

7. A meeting schedule will look like this: (modify as needed).

7:30—8:00 p.m.	Welcome, refreshments, sharing questions
8:00—8:30	Bible study and application
8:30—9:00	Sharing and prayer

8. We will have the following rules concerning:
   - Homework
   - Refreshments
   - Childcare
   - Being absent
   - Being available
   - Being confidential

3 The Support Group

Identify People in Need of Special Support

A support group is a specialized group for people in a special situation. Through mutual sharing, Bible study, and prayer, they seek to stand with and help each other through this problem or time in life. One church lists its support groups as follows:[15]

SUNDAY

Conquering Compulsive Behaviors: This group is for those who want to live life free of addictive and compulsive behaviors.

Career Builders Workshop: Career management through caring and Christian support. Includes experienced people speaking about résumés, interviews, and career development.

S.O.S. (Survivors of Suicide) For those who have lost a loved one to suicide.

Conquering Codependency: This support group is designed to help develop positive, healthy relationships.

MONDAY

Cancer Conquerors: Those diagnosed with cancer and their support persons will draw strength from this group.

TUESDAY

Positive Christian Singles: Great meeting with hundreds of single people.

Men at Peace: If you want to learn to manage your anger and rage, this group is for you. Meets in the Family Life Center.

LEAHS (Learning Effective Attitudes Healthfully and Serenely): A new support group for women that meets as an adjunct to Men of Peace.

Smokers Anonymous: This support group uses the twelve-step program to help people stop smoking.

Gamblers Anonymous: Support group for individuals struggling to overcome compulsive gambling habits.

WEDNESDAY

Conquering Fear of Success: A twelve-step program designed to help you be successful in all of your chosen life pursuits.

Alcoholics Anonymous: A twelve-step program to overcome alcohol abuse.

THURSDAY

Overeaters Anonymous: Meets weekly from 6:30–7:30 a.m.

Spatula: A support group for parents of gay children.

Women Who Love Too Much: Learn to break the pattern of relating in an unhealthy way. Share and grow with other women who have been hurt in relationships.

Fresh Start: Provides support and friendship for single mothers facing the challenge of raising their children alone.

COCOON (Children of Abuse Can Overcome Obstacles Now): A unique support group for parents whose children have been abused.

Offer an Empathic Listening Ear

It is important for the leader of a support group to empathize with the felt needs of the members. It is helpful if the leader has experienced help in the area of the groups felt need. This is not a requirement, however, as those who are experiencing difficulty will appreciate the compassion of one who facilitates a group and comes to their side with a listening ear.

Leaders of support groups need to be person-oriented. They must be available to individual members of the group when they are experiencing special difficulty or joy.

Gather the Group

Support groups form in two primary ways. The first is by personal invitation. Make a list of people who share a common need. Invite them personally, by phone, or by letter to an exploratory meeting. After a time of fellowship ask, "What brought you to this meeting? If we would continue to meet, why would we do so?"

A second way of beginning a support group is to sponsor a public seminar or kick-off meeting in the community on the subject of the felt need. Bring in an outside professional. Advertise it in the newspapers. Encourage church members to bring friends. At the event, announce that there will be a series of follow-up sessions. Indicate that the purpose of these sessions will be to give those with similar experience an opportunity to fellowship together, study relevant materials, and support each other with prayer, concern, and response. Have a response card so seminar attenders can indicate interest. Bring together in natural clusters those who express interest and explore a covenant.

Agree to a Covenant

The covenant of a support group is similar to that of a nurture group. You may want to use the Our Group Covenant form to help the group come to an agreement on who and what they want to be. Modifications might include:

1. The purpose of our group is (check one or more) to —
    _____ get to know one another.
    _____ support one another around a common concern.
    _____ reach out to others with the same concern.
    _____ explore the resources of Scripture and knowledgeable persons.
    _____ mature in Christ by adopting a common discipline.
    _____ other

2. Our specific objectives or hopes are. . . .

3. Resources to be used will include. . . .

Support groups generally agree to meet together for six to eight sessions and then decide about further meetings. Some groups are ongoing. Others meet once a month or less for continuing accountability. If the group decides it has either failed or succeeded in its objective and is no longer needed, it needs to share the benefits received from the experience and disband.

Begin with the Felt Need

Unlike a basic nurture group, whose members begin by introducing themselves generally, support group members need to tell their story from the perspective of the felt need that brought the group together. For example, an Alcoholic Anonymous group begins with someone telling a personal story in relationship to alcohol abuse.

A typical meeting schedule for a support group might be:

Opening
- Introductions and refreshments
- Testimony/story of one member on rotation basis

Study
- One lesson in the study program
- Sharing and practical application

Prayer
- Prayers of thanks and gratitude
- Prayer for each person by name

After adjournment
- More coffee and informal conversation

Serendipity House is developing a rather complete set of resources for use by support groups. Materials currently available include:[16]

Special Needs
Dealing with Grief and Loss
Mid-Life: The Crises That Brings Renewal
Compassion Fatigue: Worn Out from Caring
Unemployed/Unfulfilled: The Most Difficult Job
Single Again: Life After Divorce

Marriage Enrichment
Newly Married: How to Have a Great First Year
The Golden Years: Myths and Realities of Aging
Infertility: Coping with the Pain of Childlessness
Remaining Married: Learning to Deal with Issues
Engaged: Are You Fit to be Tied?

Parenting
Parenting Adolescents: Easing the Way
Blended Families: Yours, Mine, Ours
Single Parenting: Flying Solo
Learning Disabilities: Parenting the Misunderstood
Parenting Preschoolers

Recovery
12 Steps: The Path to Wholeness
Addictive Lifestyles
Adult Children of Alcoholics
Codependency: Learning to Say Enough
Eating Disorders: When Food Is the Enemy

For further reading and resources on support groups, see *Support Groups,* by Lyman Coleman, (Littleton, Colo.: Serendipity House, 1991).

Self-disclosure
An Application Exercise

Self-disclosure is the key to closeness in a group. The more you can know about each other's situations and feelings, the more helpful you can be to each other. But self-disclosure is risky! How deep did your sharing go in today's meeting? Study the following five levels of communication, then indicate what depth-level you reached.

_____ **LEVEL 1: Cliché Conversation.** Such communication is safe. Topics include the weather, family, and friends. We use such words and phrases as, "How are you?" Or "I like your shirt."

_____ **LEVEL 2: Sharing Information and Facts.** In level 2 we talk about events, ideas, and facts but not ourselves. We might say, "At the youth sponsors meeting, they decided to sponsor a seminar on teen pregnancy."

_____ **LEVEL 3: Sharing Ideas and Opinions.** This is where some real communication begins. We might say, "If the teens would just realize chastity is the only way to go, we wouldn't have all these problems."

_____ **LEVEL 4: Sharing Feelings.** At this level we communicate how we feel about the facts, ideas, and opinions. We might dare to share, "I am really worried about my daughter. She has been staying out pretty late with Rod. I'm not sure of what is happening between them."

_____ **LEVEL 5: Sharing Complete Emotional and Personal Truth.** We take the risk of being rejected because of what we share. Self-disclosure involves a deep sense of openness and transparency. We might say, "John and I have really been depressed and discouraged. Sally came into our room Tuesday night and told us she is pregnant."

What is one barrier keeping you from sharing at a deeper level?

4 The Evangelistic Group

Get Excited About Evangelism

An evangelistic Care Group is primarily for non-Christians. Of the different Care Groups, there is probably none as exciting as one involving non-Christians. This is especially true when participants have had little contact with the church. Their insights are often refreshing, their questions provocative, and their responses surprising.

The purpose of an evangelistic Care Group is to give the participants both an experience of honest Christian fellowship and a relationship with Jesus Christ. After fellowship has been established, you will pray for an opportunity to introduce the group members to Jesus Christ and invite them to become members of the Christian family.

A home fellowship group is perhaps the best way to witness to non-Christians in our culture. Paul Miller emphasizes, "Christian fellowship does have evangelistic power. Many Christians do not realize this. They have been conditioned to think that preaching draws persons to Christ, that Christian service exemplifies Christ, that Christian worship has drawing power, and that verbal Christian testimony convinces men and points them to Christ. But many have never been told that the mere presence of Christ among his own has a magnetic pull upon an unsaved person coming into that group." [17]

When coming to a Christian Care Group, non-Christians will be looking for a difference. Miller is probably right when he says, "The average honest unsaved person knows full well how much or how little unity other groups of persons can achieve. He knows that beneath the respectable and suave surface lurk many bickerings, jealousies, and backbitings. He knows how corrupt politics can be, how petty the elite social club can be, how snobbish the fraternity can be, how coarse and uncouth the tavern group can be, how untrue to one another business partners can be, and how powerless education and culture have been to redeem man from his self-centeredness." [18]

Jesus believed that the unity a Christian group demonstrates can be such an astounding thing that the watching world will believe in the One who is so marvelously changing lives. They will know you are Christians by your love, Jesus told his disciples (John 13:35).

Nonbelievers need to see the church as the accepting, forgiving, caring community God meant it to be. These qualities will invite observers to meet the Christ who makes the qualities possible. It is easier for nonbelievers to see the dynamics of Christ at work in a group than in one person's life alone.

Miller warns that the power of fellowship evangelism needs to be used responsibly. "Group pressure to conform is a powerful thing. It is easier to change individuals when they are formed into a group than to change one of them separately." [19]

Plan Your Strategy

An evangelistic Care Group is generally formed by personal invitation. Is there another concerned person or couple in your church that you believe has a nonbelieving neighbor or a friend who is out of fellowship with Christ? Get together with that concerned person or couple to pray. Think of others who might have a nonchurched friend, family member, neighbor, or co-worker whom they might bring to a group meeting. A rule for being part of an evangelistic Care Group is that you must bring a noncommitted person with you. There should be a fifty-fifty balance between believers and nonbelievers.

Gather the Christian core of the proposed group for a meeting to clarify your purpose and plan. Seek to answer these statements:

1. The purpose of our group is. . . .
2. Our process for inviting our friends will be. . . .
3. Materials or passages for study will be. . . .
4. We will meet for _____ weeks from __ p.m. to __ p.m.
5. We will meet at _____ (place).
6. The ground rules for our group will include:
   - We will each bring a nonbeliever.
   - Our love will be unconditional.
   - Anything said in the meeting will be confidential.
   - New persons will be allowed until the third meeting.

Choose materials appropriate to the group. You might want to examine the following with your cohost. Have them on hand for your first meeting.

- Michael Green, *Who Is This Jesus?* (Toronto: Hodder and Stoughton, 1990).
- Leighton Ford, *Meeting Jesus*, A Lifeguide Bible Study (Downers Grove, Ill.: InterVarsity Press, 1988).
- M. Kunz and C. Schell, *They Met Jesus*, A Neighborhood Bible Study (Wheaton, Ill.: Tyndale House, 1971).
- Lyman Coleman, *Mark: Basic Bible Studies*, (Littleton, Colo.: Serendipity House, 1989).

Invite Your Friends

As Christians, we desire that every person in our community be in some kind of Christ-centered fellowship. We desire this not for our good but theirs. Pastors and friends should freely refer those out of fellowship with Christ to an appropriate Care Group so these people will have the opportunity to experience the meaning of life and fellowship Christ can give.

Lay leaders like you are often in a better position to invite and relate to non-Christians than are pastors. You often have more nonchurch contacts in your work. You are able to identify common concerns and speak a common language. Just as a pastor cannot do all the ministry needed in a church, so pastors and evangelists cannot do all the evangelism needed in a community. The challenge is for people like you to take the lead in bringing them together in a group and then bringing them to a relationship with Christ.

After you have discussed your purpose and strategy with your pastor, invite persons God has placed on your hearts to your home for a meal or an evening dessert. Be honest about the invitation. Tell them you would like to have an opportunity to have some relaxed fellowship and to explore meeting regularly for several weeks to examine Jesus and his relevance for life today.

Richard Peace says, "The crucial factor with an invitation is honesty. Never trick a person into coming to an evangelistic group. Not only is manipulation not the loving way to act, it will create tension during the group session. You might get a response like, 'John, you invited Marge and me to dinner. You didn't tell us that you invited all your Christian buddies as well, and that we were supposed to study the Bible afterward!' " [20]

Peace goes on to say, "When you are forthright in your invitation, your non-Christian friends, by accepting it, are committing themselves to serious participation in the group. They did

45

not have to accept. But they did. They came because they wanted to." [21]

Recognize, however, that non-Christians will find it hard to accept an invitation. They may feel threatened by the subject, the newness of the setting, and the unfamiliarity of the people. This is why non-Christians must constitute the majority in your group. You do not need a large group. Three or four are enough to begin.

Be Clear but Flexible

A covenant with non-Christians may need to be more flexible and informal than a covenant with a nurture Care Group. Seven weeks is often a good length of time for a beginning group. It takes about that many sessions to explore the basics of Christ and the Christian faith. If your guests are insecure, plan for only four weeks or simply suggest, "How about getting together another time to explore this further?"

When you gather, be clear about the purpose of your group. You might say, "How about studying the Gospel of Mark? If we do that, I suggest we study a chapter a week and try to answer the question, 'Who is this man Jesus?' Let's allow the Bible to speak for itself by reading it and simply asking, 'What does it say?' "

Make a promise to the group members that you will be:

• Regular. This group has priority for you.

• Available. You care about each one.

• Confidential. You will not share any private information without first asking permission.

Invite the potential group members to meet regularly. Explore the best place to meet. Would they like to come back to your house or rotate to each other's homes? Informally discuss ground rules concerning food, children, preparation, and visitors. Use Our Group Covenant as a behind-the-scenes checklist.

Plan Your Meeting

A typical meeting schedule might include:

Welcome
- Refreshments
- Personal sharing and caring
- Prayer for the members and meeting

Study
- One chapter (be clear about what you will do and do it)
- Identify the decision the passage calls for

After adjournment
- More coffee and personal caring
- Explore other things that you can do together

Take the Lead in Showing Acceptance

As a leader of an evangelistic Care Group, your first responsibility is to take the lead in showing acceptance, genuineness, and empathy.

Acceptance is communicated through unconditional love. No matter what the people you invite wear, say, or do, they must feel loved and cared for! This will call for sensitivity. It may mean putting out an ashtray.

Genuineness is crucial. Richard Peace says, "Failure to be honest is probably the greatest hindrance to easy and natural conversational witness." [22] As leader you need to set the pace in sharing your darker side. You need to develop a transparent personality. It is in sharing both your dreams and your failures that you show the effect of Christ on your life.

Empathy is communicated through careful listening to both a person's words and feelings. When we connect with another person's feelings, the walls of separation come down. Christians and non-Christians alike listen and respond when we pay attention to what is on their minds and hearts.

Acceptance, genuineness, and empathy are the watchwords of good counseling and therapy. Your Christian Care Group adds a new dimension to these qualities. You are not merely interacting with each other, you are meeting and interacting with God who makes the acceptance, genuineness, and empathy possible! The presence of this mysterious but powerful third personality vitally affects the group's spirit. Before leading a group, you as leader need to prepare yourself spiritually. Without God's Spirit, the divine mystery of the group will be absent.

Share Your Faith

After an accepting, caring atmosphere has been established and you have become friends, you as leader need to take the lead in sharing your faith. Be prepared to share your testimony or bits of it when it is appropriate. Most of all, help the nonbelievers develop an interest in knowing more about Jesus Christ. Take the lead in exploring the life of Christ. Allow yourself to be evangelized by learning more about Jesus.

Don't let leading an evangelistic Care Group scare you! Evangelism is simply doing for persons *outside* the church things we usually do for each other *in* the church. In both cases we begin with a person's need. Take seriously the words of Jesus, "I was hungry and you gave me something to eat" (Matt. 25:35).

Caring includes wanting our friends to know the facts of the gospel. Your task is to help the nonbelievers in the group discover for themselves what you have experienced. In some way or other you will want to communicate that:

- God loves them and has a purpose for their lives.
- Our selfishness and sin separate us from God, his love and purpose.
- Salvation, love, purpose and hope are experienced as

we confess our condition and receive forgiveness.
- God becomes real in the context of a relationship with Jesus Christ and his followers.[23]

For many of us, the dialogue which takes place in a group is a more comfortable way of talking about Christ than is one-on-one conversation. In the context of fellowship we can both demonstrate and speak of the genuine, long-lasting, caring relationships Christ makes possible.

Relaxed, flexible, and friendly will need to be your pattern. But seek to have each meeting lead toward some kind of a decision. Seek to assess the level of your group members' spiritual development. Eight levels have been identified.[24]

- Indifference Level—needs to be stirred. The boat needs to be rocked for change to come.
- Hostility Level—needs to be loved. Listen! Learn all you can.
- Ignorance Level—needs to be taught. Teach him/her the facts of Jesus.
- Interest Level—needs to be cultivated. Continue to sow the seed.
- Conviction Level—needs to be guided to Christ. Explain salvation.
- Conversion Level—needs to respond. Encourage confession and belief.
- Growing Level—needs to be encouraged. Disciple him or her.
- Serving Level—needs a ministry. Help discern his or her gift.

Jesus helped the woman of Samaria by showing acceptance, genuine personal regard, and empathy. Through good dialogue he stirred her response. The challenge for you as an evangelistic Care Group leader is to provide a good climate and dialogue so each participant can discover the truth about themselves and about Christ and the Christian faith.

Before you conclude a meeting, make a non-pressured invitation to respond. Be open and even moderately enthusiastic about wanting group members to know Jesus Christ! Be excited about what a personal relationship with Jesus and his people can mean. Share how Christ has brought you fellowship in place of loneliness, forgiveness in place of guilt or shame, purpose in place of emptiness, and hope in place of despair!

Don't be afraid to ask such questions as, "Do you understand who Jesus is? Do you know what he can do for you? Is there any reason you don't want to begin a relationship with him?" If there is openness, invite members to meet with you one-on-one. Be prepared to help them pray honestly. Be their servant and think of what might be best for them in the long run.

Stop a meeting when you agreed to stop. Don't run overtime or overstay your welcome! But don't be afraid to invite group members to a worship service, a new type of group, or to a new cycle of studies.

If you are not prepared to begin an evangelistic Care Group, work extra hard at opening your nurture, support, or mission group to new people. Paul Yonggi Cho challenges each of his home Bible study groups to set a goal of adding four new people per year. When a group reaches fifteen, it divides. Each new groups then seeks to add another four. Is it surprising that the church Yonggi pastors is the largest and fastest growing church in the world?[25]

For further guidance on beginning and leading an evangelistic Care Group, read *Small Group Evangelism* by Richard Peace (Downers Grove, Ill.: InterVarsity Press, 1985); *The Master Plan of Evangelism* by Robert E. Coleman (Old Tappan, N.Y.: Spire Books, 1964); and *Successful Home Cell Groups* by Paul Yonggi Cho (South Plainfield, N.J.: Bridge Publishing, 1981).

Networks

An Application Exercise

For each of your various networks, list two or three non-churched persons with whom you have contact.

Your Family Network
1.
2.
3.

Your Work Network
1.
2.
3.

Your Neighborhood Network
1.
2.
3.

Your Friendship Network
1.
2.
3.

Go over your name list and indicate what you think is each person's primary need.

In your training group give each other feedback in regard to your lists and observations. Discuss possible next steps or options for inviting your friends to become part of a group.

5 The Mission Group

Be Committed to Do Christ's Work

A mission Care Group is more task-oriented than other groups. Its purpose is to go beyond the needs of group members to care for some specific need in the world. "A mission group," says Gordon Cosby, pastor of Church of the Saviour in Washington, D.C., "is a small group of people (five to twelve) conscious of the action of the Holy Spirit in their lives, enabling them to hear the call of God through Christ, to belong in love to one another, and to offer the gift of their corporate life for the world's healing and unity." [26]

Sometimes the difference between a mission group and a committee may not be great. A committee with a meaningful purpose and a good level of interpersonal relationships is on the way to being a mission group. The challenge may be to bring a new quality of community to the committee. From "committee to community" is an important theme for established church programs.

A mission group seeks to minister to its members before expecting them to minister to others. It has both an internal and an external agenda. Elizabeth O'Connor has termed these agendas the *inward* and the *outward* journeys. During the first minutes of its meeting, a mission group looks inward, seeking to meet needs of its members. Then it looks outward to its task.

In one sense, everyone needs to be converted three times. The first conversion brings us into personal relationship with God through Jesus Christ. It is usually characterized by a desire to spend personal time with God through Bible reading and prayer.

The second conversion brings us into relationship with each other in Christ's body. It calls us to pray and to read the Bible with each other.

The third conversion is to Christ's work. It causes us to turn from ourselves and from each other to a relationship with the world. It calls us to pray for and to serve the world in obedience to Jesus Christ. A careful balance and fullness of these three dimensions is necessary for us to be fully mature and equipped for ministry.

The three conversions or commitments can be visualized as a series of three stairs. Our commitment is to:

Christ's work
—Pray for the mission
—Study and do God's will

Christ's body
—Prayer for each other
—Study Bible together

Christ
—Personal prayer
—Bible reading

Sound a Call

A mission group comes into being when a person is gripped by a need in the church or world and sounds a call for response. At the Church of the Saviour, which has modeled mission groups for over thirty years, a group becomes reality when at least three people respond to the call and their covenant is affirmed by the pastor or approving board.

Gordon Cosby says that "the person's call may be shared with the Sunday morning congregation or with any segment of the community. . . . If others respond, they begin their life together, evoking one another's gifts, and praying for clarity in hearing God's will as to their mission. If the new group lives and senses God in its midst, it may share its call with the church council to see if it is confirmed by the representatives of the existing mission groups. This serious testing of call is extremely important." [27]

Calls to care are as broad as the world. You might experience a call to respond to the needs of foreign students, to open a youth center, or to begin a self-help store. Calls might address specific situations related to poverty, racism, loneliness, or violence. Whatever it is, the call must come out of deep conviction and felt need.

Kennon L. Callahan observes that "missional outreach does not normally come forth from planning retreats, board meetings, or long-range planning committees. More often than not, mission simply grows itself up because a small number of people—three to five—have discovered similar longings to help with a specific human hurt and hope. Growing from their longings, that missional outreach blossoms and develops into a full-range mission in the community." [28]

The First United Methodist Church of Tulsa, Oklahoma, lists its mission groups as follows:[29]

- **Legal Counseling Ministry**—offers legal services and counseling for persons in need of legal assistance.
- **Used Car Ministry**—acquiring used or broken-down cars, repairing them, and donating them to persons in need of such.
- **Ministry to the Hearing Impaired**—providing interpretation of Sunday worship services and offering fellowship opportunities to the hearing impaired of our community.
- **Jobs First**—providing job placement services; matching the skills of un-

employed persons with known job openings; assisting in résumé preparations.

- **Odd Jobs Ministry**—doing a variety of tasks and repairs for persons unable to do such for themselves.
- **Ministry with the Poor, Hungry, and Homeless**—provides food, clothing, and shelter for families and individuals.
- **Prison Ministry**—visiting, counseling families, and providing worship services and Bible studies for those who are incarcerated.
- **Aviation Ministry**—providing transportation by way of private airplane for persons in need of such.
- **Tutoring Ministry with Adults**—teaching illiterate adults to read and write through the structure of the Literacy Center.
- **Ministry with Unwed Mothers**—sponsoring a Maternity Clothes Closet in our church which supplies maternity wear and infant items to mothers in need.
- **Jewish-Christian Relations Ministry**—working to strengthen Jewish-Christian relationships through education, communication, and cooperation.
- **Meals on Wheels**—providing residential delivery of hot, nutritious lunches to persons unable to prepare their own meals.
- **Ministry with the Elderly**—visiting elderly community members who live in nursing homes or are homebound.
- **Christian Medical Clinic**—offering medical care (through the Great Physician Mobile Medical Clinic) for those who cannot pay.
- **Adopt-A-Family**—partnering with families on a short-term basis in order to help them assess and work through their needs.
- **Christian Financial Ministry**—providing counsel and information for persons in financial crisis and for those who wish to learn to live within a budget.
- **Christian Business Ministry**—providing support and fellowship for business persons wanting to establish their businesses on Christian principles.

Clarify the Basics

When a call is given to begin a mission group, a time and place to discuss it should be agreed on. At this first meeting, the key agenda will be to clarify and write out the call.

A call, like a purpose statement, generally seeks to answer the questions, "What are we seeking to do?" "Whom are we seeking to do it for?" and "Why do we want to do it?" An example would be, "We will offer legal services and counseling [what], for persons in need of legal assistance [who], so they can experience the justice and the invitation to faith we believe God wants for them [why].

A mission group, like a nurture group, needs to agree on basic questions, such as, "When and where will we meet?" "What will a typical schedule look like?" "What about refreshments, guests, and children?" (You might want to use the worksheet Our Group Covenant to guide your discussion).

Finances may need to be addressed in your covenant. A rule of thumb for some mission groups is to challenge their members to voluntarily tithe their finances and their time toward the mission. Some can give more, others less. An important principle is that "the real responsibility, including determination of strategy, securing of staff, and raising of funds, must be placed squarely upon the mission group embodying the call."[30]

Hold the Call and Discern the Gifts

The key role of a mission group leader is to *sound* and *hold* a call. This is what brings the group into being and holds it together. The leader needs to take responsibility for clearly articulating the call and keeping it before the group. If a call is not reinforced, individuals can lose a vision within mere weeks.

When you experience a call to mission, you have a focus around which your group forms. One of the first items of business when your group meets will be, "Who will do what?" You will be pondering what tasks need to be done and who has the gift or ability for each particular task.

God gives to an authentic mission group all the gifts it needs. But the gifts need to be discerned. If a person's gift is not identified, the person will probably experience feelings of inferiority, envy, or bitterness. The leader and group need to take seriously the observation of the apostle Paul that "to each one the manifestation of the Spirit is given for the common good" (1 Cor. 12:7).

As leader of a mission group, your task is to see that both nurture and mission happen. Your task is to serve as moderator of the group and delegate various leadership tasks to others in the group. You should not lead Bible studies or perform other major functions if you are not gifted for these.

As with the nurture, support, and evangelistic groups, your role as a leader is to be a servant of the group. You need to convene the meetings, lead a good dialogue, make sure all points of view are heard, delegate responsibilities according to the gifts of members, and ensure that there is good follow-through of decisions made. Part three of this handbook will give more helps and guidelines on leadership issues.

Attend to Inward and Outward Agendas

The Church of the Saviour insists that "the outward journey is possible only as an expression of the inward. Unless the inward issues in the outward, the effort turns in on itself and destroys its pilgrims." [31] The inner needs of your members can be met by leading in a time of fellowship and sharing (see chapter 6). They can be met via a brief Bible study that fits your situation (see chapter 7). They can be met through a time of prayer in which the needs of each member are specifically remembered (see chapter 8).

Be clear with the group or committee concerning how much time you are planning to give to inward journey agenda and how much you will give to outward journey agenda. Some groups spend half their meeting time in sharing-study-prayer and the other half in planning their mission or doing their committee work. You will need to decide. A good balance between the inward and outward journeys is vital.

Discover the Resources Needed

To begin listing resources for mission groups would be a mammoth task. Each mission group will be unique and require its own set of resources. When a call is experienced, there is joy in visualizing an appropriate response to a need. But often a feeling of despair follows which says, "It is not possible." Hope again emerges when the group members come together and share resources. Trust your members and the resources God gives to them.

Conclude with Honor

There is no average length of time for membership in a mission group. Experienced people say, "One may be in a group for a few months or for fifteen years or longer. Each member is encouraged to be open to God's call on her life. A deepening understanding of God's call and a deepening awareness of her gifts may lead the member into new dimensions of mission in her original group. Her call may be of long duration, even for a lifetime." [32]

An annual review of groups by the congregation's board or council of elders is appropriate. Each group or committee leader should bring an annual statement of the group's purpose to the board or even to the congregation, giving a reason why the group should continue to exist. If the committee or group's purpose has been met, the group should be encouraged to celebrate what God has done and go on to other things.

Our Group's Purpose
An Application Exercise

Definite purpose is the starting point of all achievement. An articulate purpose statement becomes a good measuring stick for evaluating the call, direction, and progress of a group. Use the following what, who, and why questions to write or revise the purpose statement of your present group.

1. What do we want to accomplish?

2. Who are the people that will benefit?

3. Why are we hoping to do this?

With the above as background experience, write a purpose statement in the triangle for the group you hope to lead.

Purpose Statement

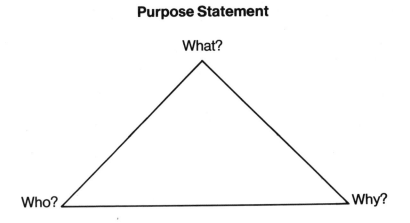

PART III Basic Elements

Four basic elements are present in a healthy Care Group. These are acceptance which leads to fellowship, Bible study which leads to insight, sharing which leads to prayer, and discussion of needs which leads to mission.

These four elements of group life might be diagramed as a baseball diamond. If the members of your Care Group experience acceptance, you have made it to first base. If a clear lesson has been learned, the group has reached second base. Third base is achieved when group members have shared their feelings with each other and with God. And the group has scored when it has been faithful in mission!

The Care Group Diamond

Lesson learned
(Bible study)

Feelings expressed
(Prayer)

Acceptance experienced
(Fellowship)

Mission accomplished
(Mission)

The next four chapters will examine these four basic elements.

Group life is like walking a tightrope. To stay alive, you need to keep your balance! Groups that emphasize only acceptance become shallow, causing members to look elsewhere for meaning to life. If study is overemphasized, the group becomes academic and duplicates school or Sunday school experiences. The sharing of feelings and prayer without mission is like racing a car engine without putting it in gear.

If time consistently runs out for one aspect of the meeting, change the order. For example, after the sharing question, begin with prayer instead of Bible study or go directly into the discussion of your mission. Maintaining balance is vital to the health and vitality of a group.

New members bring fresh challenges to a group. There is a new need for acceptance. New insights, feelings, and needs will stir the group to new growth.

Challenge your group to do its best to add a new person or couple during each term that it meets. When a group reaches nine or more persons, it should break into fours for Bible study or commission several members to begin a new group.

6 Acceptance

Accept Each Member

A major goal of a Care Group is to have each member of the group enjoy good fellowship. For this to happen, each must experience personal acceptance. Personal acceptance occurs when there is unconditional personal regard. It happens when you treat another as an equal no matter how the person looks, feels, or acts.

Acceptance is another word for grace or unmerited favor. It is given as a gift. As leader, you need to offer acceptance to each person and seek to have members of the group offer it to each other.

A good group meeting begins when the first member arrives. As leader you should meet all persons on their arrival. Shake hands warmly. Establish eye contact. Ask how the week has gone and how their family, work, or the concern shared at a previous meeting are fairing. Listen carefully. Respond in a caring way. Be a pastor to your people! Focus on people and their concerns, not on study materials or details.

Acceptance also happens as people position themselves in relationship to others. No second rows in a Care Group! Help members sit in a tight circle. If possible, sit close enough so you can hold hands in the circle. Pull chairs or even couches inward. Removing distance between people increases closeness. Make sure each person can see every other person. Avoid having three persons on a couch.

Use people's names as often as possible. Frequent use of names builds a sense of belonging and connectedness. It also helps others in the group learn names quickly. Names are important to a people-oriented group!

Share Your Life Histories

Acceptance in a group comes from being known. Some groups get off to a good start by asking each individual or couple to take an evening to tell their life story. Have them share their roots. Ask them about the significant people, places, and milestones of the past. Have them share current values, relationships, joys, and anxieties. Some individuals have found it helpful to draw and share a graph of their spiritual journey.

Be thorough but do not let anyone ramble. Go for understanding! As a person shares, ask yourself, "Who is this person and how did he or she come to be this way? How far along the road is he or she toward fulfilling God's plans and call?"

If you do not share life stories in depth, take extra time during the first four or five sessions to get to know each other and build community in other ways. When a new person joins the group, stop to get to know the person. Have all members again briefly introduce themselves. From the beginning, put the emphasis on persons rather than academics.

"Go heavy on group building at first!" is Lyman Coleman's wise counsel, outlined in his Serendipity materials.[33] As the group matures, spend progressively more time in Bible study and mission. A general rule is to spend twice as much time in fellowship at the beginning of a group's life as you spend at the end. This might be diagramed as follows:

A Group's Use of Time

	Sept	Oct	Nov	Dec	Jan	Feb	Mar	Apr	May	June
Bible study										
Fellowship and sharing (2/3 of the time at first; 1/3 at the end)										
Mission										

Ask a Sharing Question

Begin each regular meeting with a sharing question. It will get all members involved in dialogue and personal sharing from the very beginning! Allow fifteen or twenty minutes.

A good sharing question has at least five key qualities.

- It is simple and specific. It can be answered in three or four sentences. For example, "What was your 'high' for the week and how did it make you feel?"
- It links a request for factual information with feelings related to those facts such as: "Where did you live when you were seven and who in your family were you closest to at the time?"
- It can be answered by everyone in the group. Don't ask "Tell us about your baptismal experience," if there is a nonbaptized person in the group!
- It is an open rather than a closed question. In other words, it does not call for a yes or no answer.
- It asks for the sharing of self, not the sharing of an opinion or information related to some incident or theory.

If possible, a sharing question should have some connection with the main point of the study or purpose of the meeting. During the first weeks of a group, try to ask past tense questions that invite participants to share something about their personal history. Then move to present tense questions that help them share what is happening in their lives now. After your group has been together for a while, ask future tense questions about hopes, dreams, and desires for change.

Examples of sharing questions might include:

- What family trip stands out in your mind and why?
- What did you appreciate in your father and how has that affected you?
- What was your "high" or your "low" for the week?
- What do you do on a typical Wednesday?
- What do you like best and least about your job?
- If you knew you could not fail, what would you like to try in the next year?
- What is one change you would like to make in your life in the next year?
- Where would you like to be and what would you like to be doing five years from now?

Make the time of sharing relaxed and enjoyable. Ask a question and call on a braver member to answer. Then move to the right around the circle, allowing people to "pass" if they cannot or do not want to answer the question. Do not ask follow-up questions of the speaker or you will run out of time. Do not ask questions which require people to confess their sins or say negative things about themselves. If confession occurs, it should be voluntary, not coerced.[34]

Listen Actively

Your most important task from the time the first person arrives at your meeting is to listen! At the end of the meeting, what you have heard is more important than what you have said.

Active listening more than anything else will tell your group members that you care about them and what is happening in their lives. Active listening tells them that you want to know them as persons. You want to know their thoughts and experiences. You want to know their feelings. You want your members to know that they have value in your eyes just as you have value in Gods eyes!

"It is impossible to overemphasize the immense need humans have to be really listened to," says Paul Tournier.[35] Even when people are surrounded by family and friends, they are often not being listened to. People are helped to grow, to develop confidence, and to feel loved by being listened to. "The ear is the most powerful part of the human body," says Lee Griess of Stephen Ministries. "People are healed by the laying on of ears." [36]

We listen because God first listened to the cry of the Hebrews and then to our cry. We want to do for others what he has done for us. Because of God's care for us, we are enabled and made willing to care for others. We love because he first loved us! (1 John 4:19).

Learning to listen is a must for any Care Group leader. Draw out those who have fallen into silence and listen to a speaking person until they feel heard. Sometimes listening may need to take place outside of group time.

Attentive listening will also bring tremendous benefits to your life. Three benefits stand out.

- *If you want to become wise,* you will need to listen. We learn about people, places, events, and important qualities by listening.
- *If you want to be liked,* you will need to listen. Your group may admire you for your brilliant teaching, your funny stories, or your skill in leading a meeting, but they will like or dislike you on the basis of how well and how deeply you listen to them.

- *If you want to be effective,* you need to listen. What you seek to do for your group members will be nearly worthless unless it is based upon their needs. To be effective, you need to know what your group members are thinking and feeling. You find out what your members need by listening to them.

Good listening is hard work. It calls for active concentration or attending. This means physically and emotionally focusing on the person who is speaking. Good listening invites persons to speak, then listens to what they have to say. Listen as you would like to be listened to! There is no shortcut. If you want to be a caring person and to have a caring group, you will need to learn how to listen. Good listening leads to deep caring for each other and for the world.

The average person can talk at about 125 words per minute. But theoretically we can listen at the rate of about 350 or 400 words per minute.[37] If you are truly attentive, your mind can use that gap between 125 words and 400 to analyze what is being said. In addition to hearing the words, your mind can be attentive to the person's feelings. What emotions are evident? Is the person expressing joy, sadness, hope, despair? Is the person tense or relaxed? What do the person's mannerisms, eyes, clothes, and words tell you?

Respond Reflectively

As a good listener, you need to respond to what you hear. Sometimes just a nod will show you are listening. At other times you may need to restate something in your own words.

Words can mean different things to different people. As a good listener, you need to verify that you have understood what has been said. For example, I can say, "I was raised on a farm." You may think you understand. But what does "farm" mean to you? For some it means a berry or truck farm. For others it means a dairy or poultry farm. For still others it means a five thousand-acre ranch. Such differences of meaning are possible with almost every statement we make!

To give permission for a person to go deeper, we often need to clarify the previous statement. We might ask, "Can you clarify that for me?" or "Could you describe the problem a bit more?" Such responses will help the group get a more complete picture and help the person speaking to explore further his or her problem, reasoning, and/or possible options.

To show that you understand how a member of your group is feeling about an issue or her situation, you can respond to a statement by saying, "You seem to feel pretty _____ [happy, sad, angry] about that. What do you think might be done?" Ask open-ended questions that can not be answered with a simple yes or no. Then listen to what is said and seek to lead it a step deeper.

Use Food as a Tool

Refreshments break the ice. Food is a gift. When given a gift, participants feel accepted. With cup in hand most people are more ready to enter into conversation at the beginning of a meeting or to relax and share at the end. Beware, however, of the socially inept person. A social time can be the most agonizing of all times. If you see discomfort, go to the person's side or encourage another member to relate informally and comfortably.

Some find it best to serve refreshments at the end of the meeting so those who must rush away can leave early while those who want to talk are free to do so. Refreshments should be simple so those from a poor or simple lifestyle are not intimidated. Some groups say, "Serve whatever you like, but keep it in a cup."

Occasionally go deeper in fellowship by doing something that goes beyond refreshments. Plan a picnic in the park or a potluck meal with an evening of games. Attend a drama, concert, or ball game together. A retreat is ideal and some would say essential. You might explore doing something extra or different on the fourth week of each month.

Listen as People Leave

Especially at the end of a group meeting, be relaxed. Don't rush home. Roberta Hestenes says, "The group is not over until the last person goes home. Often the most significant conversations will occur after the group time is finished. The leader should make every effort to stay around and talk until everyone has gone home. Sometimes questions or concerns which could not be expressed in the group will come up in the after-meeting. Someone with a question about their relationship with Jesus Christ may linger for a word of counsel. Those with a decision or problem may ask for prayer or help. Good listening is very important at this key time. Lives may be encouraged, directed, or helped by these conversations. Take them seriously." [38]

As each person leaves, you want them to feel accepted and to know that they will be received warmly again when they return next week.

For further help on building relationships in a small group and for a listing of sharing questions, see chapter 7, *Using the Bible in Groups*, by Roberta Hestenes (Philadelphia, Pa.: Westminster Press, 1983).

Sharing Questions
An Evaluation Exercise

A sharing question invites members to tell their group something about themselves. A good question encourages members to talk about past experiences, present situations, hopes for the future, joys and sorrows, struggles, and successes. It combines a statement of fact with feelings related to it.

What was today's sharing question? _____

_____

On a scale from Poor to Excellent rate the qualities of today's sharing question with an X on the line.

Poor   Fair   Good   Very good   Excellent

1. It was simple and specific.

_____

2. It could be answered by everyone.

_____

3. It was an open rather than a closed yes/no question.

_____

4. It asked for the sharing of self, not issues or ideas.

_____

5. It asked for both factual information and emotions related to it.

_____

6. It helped focus on the main point of today's study.

_____

In retrospect what would have been another sharing question that could have helped the group toward deeper fellowship and towards a focus on the main point of today's study? _____

_____

7 Bible Study

Believe in Bible Study

The Bible is our ultimate guide for faith and life. It has shaped the life of the church and its people more than any other resource throughout its long history. The Bible is a reliable record of how God has revealed himself and how people have responded. Help your group to discover who God is and to know what guidance he has for their lives.

There will be those who do not read their Bibles at home but will read them in the context of your Bible study. Let the Bible become an open book in your group. Your job as a leader is not to lecture, to teach, or to have all the answers. Your task is to help group members experience the joy of discovery.

Discovery happens best through asking questions, then nurturing a good level of dialogue around those questions. For too long the church has concentrated on one-way communication. Preaching and teaching that goes from pulpit to pew and lectern to pupil is valuable —but people also need dialogue and that is the purpose of your group.

Dialogical Bible study is open, two-way Bible study. It requires a good balance of listening and speaking. When balance is achieved, it enables your members to know one another, to know God, and to more clearly discern God's way for their lives.

Five steps can help you lead a high quality Bible study week after week. The five steps form the easily remembered acronym ABIDE.[39] (See the ABIDE worksheet at the end of this chapter, which uses this acronym to help you prepare a good Bible study. You may want to duplicate the worksheet for future use).

Have a Clear Aim

A **is for AIM.** A good leader of dialogue, like a good public speaker, begins with a clear objective or aim. An aim is a brief statement of what you want to see happen as a result of the study. Put down in writing a working statement of what you want group members to know and do when they have finished discovering the truth of the passage.

The aim should be based on the main truth of the passage. Read the passage carefully before you start filling out a study guide. What does the passage say? Outline the passage as you probably did in a high school English class. Following is an example.

They devoted themselves   Alternate Translations
  —to the apostles' teaching, and
  —to the fellowship,
  —to the breaking of bread and
  —to prayer.
Everyone was filled with awe, and many wonders
and miraculous signs were done
   —by the apostles.
All the believers were together and
  —had everything in common.
  —Selling their possessions and goods,
  —they gave to anyone
   —as he had need.

Every day <u>they</u>
    —continued to meet together in the temple courts,
    —broke bread in their homes and
    —ate together
      —with glad and sincere hearts,
      —praising God and enjoying the favor of all the people.
And <u>the Lord</u> added
    —to their number daily
    —those who were being saved. (Acts 2:42-47)

Go over the passage again. Underline the key actors. Circle the verbs. Draw lines to note repetition or relationship of words or concepts.

Read the text again in another version. In the margin, note different ways of expressing the same thought. If you do not know Greek or Hebrew, this is the best way to get a clue to the richness of meaning contained in words and phrases.

Stay with the passage until you understand its key point. What is it trying to say? Write it in your own words. Then seek to discern what that key point is saying to your group. What does it want your group to do? When you understand that, write it down! It is your aim.

A clear objective or aim will help you prepare your discussion questions or evaluate those given in a study guide. An aim will also help you evaluate progress as you proceed through the study. It will help you refocus your direction when the group gets off on a tangent. Knowing your aim will also give you and the group satisfaction when you hit the mark or get the point you believe God has for you in the passage. When Nehemiah had the Scriptures read, and the people of Israel received new guidance, Nehemiah exclaimed, "The joy of the Lord is your strength!" (Neh. 8:10).

Research the Background

B **means BACKGROUND.** Research the background of the passage. What is behind the scenes? In a Bible dictionary, read up on the places mentioned in the passage. Study the people. Explore the meaning of a key word or two. Richardson's *Word Studies of the Bible* is a helpful tool.[40]

Don't feel obligated to share all of your research. Ask questions that help group members share as much information as they know. Keep your findings as a reservoir to add to the discussion at an appropriate time. What you add should be simple, usable, and out of sight. Don't lean on outside sources during the study.

You will need to decide how much study will be expected of your group members in preparation for your meetings. How much will happen on their own and how much discovery will happen at the meeting itself?

Home study gives members an opportunity to think, to go deeper during the meeting, and to be efficient in the use of each other's time. But discovering truth separately rather than together enhances personal agenda. It makes discussion more diverse and often more difficult. *Mastering the Basics* book studies prepared by Lyman Coleman and Richard Peace do an excellent job of integrating self-study, group study, and expository public teaching.[41]

Begin with an Interesting Introduction

I invites you to write an interesting **INTRODUCTION.** Begin your study with an object, a story, an illustration, or an opening question that will lead to your aim. If the aim of a study of Acts 2:42-47 is to have the same quality of fellowship in your group as the early disciples had in theirs, you might share a personal story or invite group members to tell about a time when they "ate together with glad and sincere hearts."

After your introduction, read the text. Vary your method of reading. One week you may want to have everyone read the text in unison. The next week you might ask one member to read it aloud or you might assign parts as in a drama. Read antiphonally. Read around the circle. Do something different nearly every week!

Ask Three Main Questions

D **in the acronym ABIDE stands for DISCUSSION questions.** In advance, prepare three main questions that will progressively lead you to the aim of your study. Each main question may have follow-up questions.

The first of the three questions should be an observation question asking, **"What does the passage say?"** It will ask for basic information about the *who, what, when, where,* and *how* of the passage. For the Acts 2 passage you might ask, "Who were the 'they' in this story? What ten things did they do?" Be sure you have done your background study!

The second question should relate to interpretation. It will ask, **"What does the focal point of the passage mean?"** Help your group to *define* the terms and *explain* the relationships, significance, or consequence of the passage. What did it mean for the early believers to sell their possessions? Did that have any relationship to eating with glad and sincere hearts? Keep asking questions until you understand the main point of the passage! Keep throwing questions back to the group. Never tell the group something they can discover by your asking the right question!

The third question should be an application question. It will ask, **"What should we do?"** This question is the link between the main point and your daily lives. This is where the rubber meets the road! If you neglect this question, you will lose the message God has for your situation and not reach your aim. Application questions have to do with you, your place of work, your place of living, and how you live. You want to help your group to move beyond teaching and learning to caring and reconciliation.

For the Acts passage you might ask, "How and where might

our group experience this kind of life?" Invite specific commitments and agree to lovingly hold each other accountable.

An alternate set of study questions to the above might be:

1. What stood out for you in this passage?

2. What did this passage really say and mean to the people who first received it?

3. Can you illustrate this main point or experience from your own life?

4. What do you need from God right now to apply this lesson to your life?

Using a prepared study guide is the easiest route but not necessarily the best. If you use a prepared study guide, prepare your own aim for the study. Delete all questions not crucial to that aim! The ultimate aim of group Bible study is application, not just accumulation of knowledge. Try your best to keep the study to three main questions and lead a dialogue in relationship to them.

Practice your main questions in advance. Anticipate what the responses of your group members might be. Eliminate or change awkward or hard-to-answer questions. Think through how you might help group members dialogue with each other. How can you help them respond to and ask each other questions?

Clinch the Main Point

E in the acronym ABIDE stands for END. End your study with a climactic summary. State clearly and concisely the points the group has discovered. Then use a question, a summary, or a closing story in a way that will leave your group members with one big thought or concrete thing to do. Make this so clear that if next week you ask, "What did we learn last week and what did we agree to do?" your group members will immediately be able to tell you.

Conclude your Bible study by announcing what you will

study next week. Help the group look forward to the study by asking a motivating question about its main point. For example, "How are we going to respond to the famine in Africa? Is there anything we can do? Next week's Bible study from Luke 9:10-17 will give us some clues."

Usually the Bible study will lead to a time of prayer. The prayer will allow participants to express their feelings of praise, confession, or commitment in response to the main truth that God has impressed upon them.

For further help on how to lead a Bible study see *How to Lead Small Group Bible Studies*, edited by Navigators staff (Colorado Springs, Colo.: Navpress, 1982) and *Using the Bible in Groups*, by Roberta Hestenes, (Philadelphia, Pa.: Westminster Press, 1983).

ABIDE Bible Study Worksheet

THE PASSAGE _____

WHAT DOES IT SAY?   Alternate readings
(Outline the passage.)   in other versions

Preparation

Aim: What is the main point of the passage and what do you want your members to do about it?

Background: Behind the scenes words, places or people for further study.

_____   _____   _____

The Study

Introduction: An object, story, or opening question that will orient the group toward the main theme or aim. Read the passage.

Discussion Questions:
1. Observation: What does it say about. . . .

2. Interpretation: What did _____ mean to _____?

3. Application: What are we going to do about _____?

End: The concluding story, summary, or challenge.

Assignment

Preparation
An Evaluation Exercise

A study worksheet or outline helps a leader to prepare a good Bible study. It is to a discussion leader what a good map is to a traveler. Describe and evaluate today's Bible study using the acronym ABIDE as a guide.

AIM. What do you think was the leader's silent aim for today's Bible study? What did the leader want us to think or do when we were finished?

How well was the aim achieved?

BACKGROUND. What evidence was there that the leader had done background study before coming?

INTRODUCTION. What kind of an introduction did the leader have to the study? How did it prepare the group for the main theme or the ultimate aim of the study?

DISCUSSION QUESTIONS. What were the main discussion questions?
   1.
   2.
   3.

END. What was the question, summary, or story that helped to summarize and apply the passage to our lives?

8 Prayer

Respond to God

Prayer is our response to God. After God speaks to us through Scripture and our fellow pilgrims, it's our turn to respond to God and his will with thankfulness, confession, or new commitment.

Prayer in a Care Group can have several purposes. It can build faith and help members experience the presence of God. It can help group members feel their needs and concerns have been heard. Prayer can strengthen group relationships as members express common needs to the same God. Prayer can also enable group members to minister beyond self to others. Prayer can direct attention away from self to Jesus. Prayer can be a bridge that leads to further worship.

Prayer can be the most meaningful part of a group's time together. Leave adequate time for it. Prayer is a powerful climax to group dialogue. In prayer, participants have an opportunity to restate learnings and feelings from an eternal perspective. God is consciously and specifically drawn into the conversation. Conversing with God helps put issues, problems, and priorities in proper perspective.

Prayer is an indicator of how alive God is in our lives and in a group. Prayer is the primary way we have of communicating with God. If there is no prayer or communication, there is no personal relationship with God. Feel free to claim the promise of Jesus who said, "Where two or three come together in my name, there am I with them" (Matt. 18:20).

Clarify Basic Ground Rules

Praying together makes some people nervous and uncomfortable. It may not be something they usually do. They may be intimidated because they have heard others pray in public, polished ways. Allay fears of your Care Group members by outlining and practicing a few basic ground rules.

• Forget formal-sounding phrases. Concentrate on things you are feeling and say them in your own words.
• Don't be anxious. Directions will always be given on how prayer will begin, proceed, and end. If someone is to lead or close in prayer, they will be asked beforehand.
• You will be encouraged and helped but not pressured to pray. Prayer will always be voluntary.
• We will not spend too much time sharing prayer requests. We will let the sharing happen in the praying.

Help New People Begin

Invite people who have not previously prayed in public to utter just one word as part of a prayer that you will begin. You might explain, "Today I want to give you an opportunity to pray a prayer of thanks. Your prayer will be only one word long. I will begin by praying, 'Lord, tonight we are thankful for the Bible. . . .' and then you will be invited to mention one other thing, person, or quality for which you are thankful. Next week we will also pray one-word prayers, not only of thanks but also of confession and intercession. Today I just invite you to pray a word of thanks."

Proceed to pray:
- Lord, tonight we are thankful for the Bible and for _____
(family, health, my new job)

Next week add:
- Tonight I confess that I have been _____
(impatient, critical, lonely)
- Lord, we are concerned about _____
(name the persons for whom you have a concern)

After participating in word prayers, group members will soon feel comfortable with phrase and sentence prayers. Conversational prayer also seems like a natural sequence.

Converse with God[42]

Conversational prayer is a group of persons in conversation with each other and their heavenly Father. The praying is done in conversational tones, one theme or topic at a time, as a natural conversation. Prayers are direct, simple, brief, and to the point. They move back and forth between members of the group. Each person who prays offers just one sentence at a time related to the theme or topic. Members of the group may pray audibly as many times during the prayer time as they wish. Begin by asking the group and agreeing on the themes or topics for which you will pray.

In conversational prayer one person may pray for Greg who is ill. Another person may add another thought about Greg. A third person may pray for Greg's wife and family. Then someone may bring up a new subject and one, two, or more people may add something to that prayer. Sometimes just a word or phrase may be added. When the prayer time seems completed, the leader should close as he or she usually does.

Use a Variety of Patterns

Avoid deadly monotony! Use a variety of patterns not only for reading the Scriptures, but also during your prayer time. Here are suggestions.

1. Go around the circle asking, "How can we pray for you tonight?" Have each group member share, then encourage each to pray for one other person in the group. In your closing prayer, remember any concern or person that has been missed.

2. Pair off into prayer partners. Generally prayer partners are of the same gender and meet once a week. They agree to be open and honest with each other and to share specifically what God is trying to teach them. They avoid aimless conversation and seek to pray specifically for each other's needs and concerns. For more guidelines on prayer partners, you might want to consult InterVarsity Christian Fellowship's *Small Group Leader's Handbook*.[43]

3. Hand out written prayers or ask each person to bring or write a prayer. Read the prayers during your prayer time. Don't neglect the Bible's written prayers.

4. Pray in response to a news item. Assist your members by giving each a church bulletin or a page from a recent daily newspaper or magazine.

5. Record prayer requests and answers! After the prayer time, have someone record the prayer requests of the evening in a prayer diary. Leave room beside each request for recording answers to prayer. These can become material for further prayers of thanks, confession, and praise. A prayer diary may look something like this:

Prayer Diary

Date	Person requesting prayer and nature of the request	Date answer	Nature of the answer

Organize a Prayer Chain

A prayer chain can give your group the opportunity between meetings to pray for any individual of the group or for any concern that someone might have for intercession. Judy Hamlin has developed the following guidelines.[44] List the members with phone numbers in alphabetical or any other logical order. Give each member a copy with the following instructions on it.

Upon receiving a call remember the concern is prayer. Then pass the request on to the person below your name on the prayer-chain list. If there is no answer, keep calling down the list until someone is reached so that the chain will not be broken. At a later time, try to re-call the person(s) you missed to share the request. Do not allow the chain to break.

Do not take time to chat. Pray the requests to God. Pray fervently. Keep requests confidential. Pray for the request as long as you feel it is necessary, depending on the nature of the request.

The last person called should call the first person on the prayer-chain list, to let him or her know the chain has been completed. Call prayer answers to your prayer leader or the first person on the list.

Expand Prayer to Worship

Don't limit your worship to spoken prayers. Worship may

include praise, confession, and adoration through singing, drama, unison readings, and joyful shouts. Seek variety and balance in your prayer and worship experiences.

Singing often helps to set a mood. It assists the group in expressing its feelings to God and to each other. But be careful. Not everyone likes to sing. Be sensitive to newcomers. They can be quickly alienated by a negative experience involving singing. You might ask them about their music interests or indicate that you like to sing and invite them to listen.

If your group has a difference in musical tastes, encourage group members to sing each other's songs. Sing heartily, not necessarily because you love the music, but because you love the people who do!

Occasionally you might want to recite the Apostles' Creed in unison. Or you might read a psalm, a song, or a poem. Silence while watching a candle or the embers in a fireplace may be an occasional option. If it is affirmed by the church, observe communion together from time to time. Invite your pastor to join you for the occasion.

For more on conversational prayer read the classic *Prayer, Conversing with God* by Rosalind Rinker (Grand Rapids, Mich.: Zondervan, 1959). For a more general treatment see *Too Busy Not to Pray*, by Bill Hybels (Carol Stream, Ill.: InterVarsity Press, 1988).

Prayer

An Evaluation Exercise

Prayer should draw us into conversation with God. It should build empathy, understanding, and relationship among group members. Describe today's prayer experience.

1. What guidelines from the leader assisted you in prayer?

2. Did you feel pressure to perform?

3. What did you feel in regard to:
   - Posture. Did you sit, stand, or kneel?
   - Holding hands. Was it desired? Comfortable?
   - Time. Was prayer time adequate? Too long?
   - Silence. Were you in touch with God?
   - Content. Was it a response to God?

4. How could your prayer time have been improved?

5. Which suggestions made in the lesson would you like to explore in your group?
   - _____ Conversational prayer
   - _____ Ask each person, "How can we pray for you?"
   - _____ Pair off into prayer partners.
   - _____ Use written prayers.
   - _____ Pray in response to a news item.
   - _____ Record prayer requests and answers.
   - _____ Organize a prayer chain.

9 Mission

Be Committed to Mission

God draws people together for a purpose. That purpose is larger than study, fellowship, and prayer. Care Groups seek to go beyond teaching and learning, or even sharing and prayer, to the work of caring and reconciling.

Jesus set the model by exercising deep concern for those around him. He saw that they were "lost," "sick," "hungry," and "poor." Sometimes he meant that they were literally ill and hungry. At other times he used the terms in a figurative, spiritual sense. Whatever the situation, he came "to seek and to save what was lost" (Luke 19:10). He knew there was fundamental help available in a relationship with God and God's people.

Giving support to personal ministries and mission projects is what gives meaning and vitality to a nurture group (see chapter 2). A support group focuses its energy on helping its members and people in the community to overcome a particular difficulty (see chapter 3). An evangelistic group exists for the purpose of bringing new persons into fellowship with Christ and the church (see chapter 4). A specific mission or project is what calls a mission group into being (see chapter 5). From its beginning, Care Group members need to understand that mission is part of their life and priorities. "The first and most central characteristic of an effective, successful church is its specific, concrete missional objectives," says Kennon L. Callahan.[45] If there is no mission, the church or a group within it ceases to be what God wants it to be. On the other hand, when a group knows where it is headed and works together to accomplish its task, the group is uniquely bonded and gains a deep sense of satisfaction.

Support Members in Ministry

In the believers church tradition, every member is encouraged to be in ministry. Instead of some people doing everything, a church should encourage everybody to do something.

In the early stages of group development when the members are getting acquainted and organized, mission may primarily consist of supporting what participants are already doing outside of the group. Encourage such involvements. Help your members discern their gifts for individual mission. Support each in the ministry God has given! Personal ministries might include such challenges as:

- relating one-on-one once a week to a shut-in, a child from a broken home, or some specific needy person
- engaging in a music, speaking, or specialized ministry
- teaching a Sunday school class or being youth sponsor
- relating to people at the job with the aim of bringing reconciliation or new life in Christ
- witnessing or ministering to one person a week as the opportunity arises

At Care Group meetings, invite each member to give a brief report on their ministry. Ask one person per meeting to give a five minute report allowing you to offer encouragement (Appendix A Group Member Ministry Report may serve as a guide).

Choose a Group Project

In addition to your individual ministries, choose a group project. The project should respond to some felt need or longing in the lives of your members, then connect with a similar felt need or longing of people in the church or community.

Some groups choose a one-time project per quarter. Others choose an ongoing project to which they can give themselves week after week or month after month. Possible projects might include:

- sponsoring a monthly recreational event such as volleyball to which you can invite friends
- inviting another group for a potluck and social evening
- leading the congregation in worship by providing worship leader, Scripture reader, storyteller, musician
- sponsoring letter-writing projects directed to mission workers or important issues
- providing a monthly service at a rest home, prison facility, halfway house
- redecorating the church nursery or a run-down house or building
- sponsoring a seminar on parenting, alcohol abuse, cross-cultural relationships, or some other community need.

Take time to plan your project. Let the group brainstorm possibilities for a mission project and ways to accomplish the task. Brainstorming means that everyone suggests ideas which are recorded without comment. No one is allowed to evaluate ideas until all are listed. Then choose the three or four best possibilities and discuss pros and cons. After choosing a project, sharpen your objective, discern what needs to be done, and identify who can best do each task. Seek to have a task for everyone.

Choose to Grow

The call to make disciples calls us to grow and to help others grow in both quality and quantity. In the short-term, your mission may be personal growth, such as to understand the book of James. Each week the Bible study will lead you to grow in your understanding of God's will as you explore, "What does this passage say?" "What does it mean?" and "What are we going to do about it?" Such Bible study will eventually lead you to mission that reaches out.

You will also want to grow in the number of persons to whom you are ministering. One good pattern (as indicated in chapter 3) is to draw an empty chair into your circle at the end of the meeting. In your prayer time discuss who you would like to see in that chair next week. Give that person an invitation. Be prepared to extend a warm welcome! It is your mission.

Seek to grow another group. Aim to help plant a new Care Group. As leader, you should choose an apprentice who can occasionally lead your group. When you give birth to a new group, the apprentice can lead your group or the new one.

However you go about mission, the challenge of a Care Group is to become a group more interested in helping than being helped. An effective Care Group is more interested in loving than in being loved and prefers giving to receiving.

For further help on exploring mission, read Frank Tillapaugh's helpful book, *Unleashing the Church* (Ventura, Calif.: Regal Books, 1985).

Our Group's Mission
An Evaluation Exercise

To which base on the Care Group Diamond has your group advanced? Mark the base.

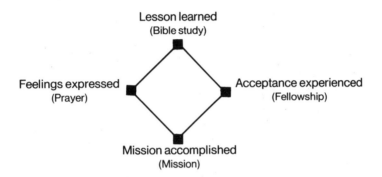

Lesson learned
(Bible study)

Feelings expressed
(Prayer)

Acceptance experienced
(Fellowship)

Mission accomplished
(Mission)

How have you progressed in your planning for mission? Indicate yes or no in response to the following eight items.

Yes No

____ ____ We agree that mission is a basic component of our group's life and purpose.

____ ____ We know, have affirmed, and prayed for the ministries of our individual members.

____ ____ We have received an in-depth report from at least one of our members concerning his or her personal mission.

____ ____ We have either brainstormed or chosen a group mission project which we are prepared to support.

____ ____ We have discerned the gifts and interests of our individual members.

____ ____ We have clear, intentional goals for our project that will help us know when we have reached our aim.

____ ____ We have bathed our mission project in prayer, seeking God's guidance and Spirit.

____ ____ TOTALS

When you think of the group you hope to lead, what thoughts do you have for the mission of the group?

PART IV Leadership Issues

Without adequate leadership, a Care Group is doomed. Doug Whallon of InterVarsity says, "Good leadership unlocks a small group's potential. Just as a good music conductor guides the orchestra into producing harmony and a football quarter back coordinates the team with a specific play to score a touchdown, so the leader of a small group helps members clarify their purpose and reach it." [46]

Leadership of a Care Group requires an understanding of group dynamics and leadership skills. It calls for an understanding of how and why people participate in groups and how their participation can be increased. Leadership requires encouragement of creativity and management of conflict.

Leadership is the unique circumstance of having followers. Both leaders and followers need to be accountable. Within supportive patterns of supervision and continuing education, leaders and followers can be a blessing to each other and can help each other effectively reach those beyond their group.

Part IV will address leadership and leadership issues from the perspective that leaders are made, not born. Leadership skills and styles will be taught. First they need to be understood. These chapters and the monthly supervision and continuing education sessions will seek to help you understand and practice the best possible leadership and ministry skills.

10 Leadership

Don't Manipulate or Force Your Way

You are being called to be part of the pastoral team of your church. As a member of that team, you will be responsible before God and your pastor for a group of people. The challenge is to help them grow spiritually and to walk with them in both the joys and struggles of life.

Leaders lead! They set the pace for those who follow. They care for their followers like a shepherd. But they do not manipulate or force their way. John Maxwell says, "Leadership is influence and influence is everything." [47] That influence needs to be under the guidance of Jesus Christ and the power of the Holy Spirit.

Leadership is a position which gives you influence. But it is more. In Jesus' day, some scribes and Pharisees had positions but were not true leaders. Leadership has to do with personality and charisma. But it is more than that. People with outstanding charisma can lead people to their ruin. Leadership also has to do with management and control. But it is much more than management of schedules and agendas.

Leadership has to do with *people* and people development!

You will want to know your people to discern their gifts and support what God wants to do through their lives.

Jesus modeled servant-leadership. Servant-leaders focus on the needs and possibilities of those entrusted to their care. As responsibility is delegated to you, you will also want to delegate responsibilities to your Care Group members once they develop the qualities and skills to handle them. Jesus gave up position and power to become an available and personal servant leader. Through personal relationships, Jesus helped people make decisions that were best for them and helpful to God. Follow in Jesus' steps.

Seek the Needed Qualities

If not accompanied by qualities of character, success and achievement will leave a person disappointed and empty. Jesus helped his disciples first to develop qualities of character, then he commissioned them to win the world to God's way of living.

Five qualities are essential for leading a Care Group. No one will be appointed as a Care Group leader who does not have some measure of these five qualities. If you do not have them, join a Care Group or work with a mentor who can help you develop them.

A Care Group leader must be:

1. *Hospitable.* Christian leaders are warm and friendly. They are open to new people. They are known for their love (John 13:35).

2. *Respected.* Care Group leaders need to be people of integrity. They can be trusted to do what they say (1 Tim. 3:1-7).

3. *Sensitive.* Good leaders are sensitive to the needs of their followers. They are filled with the Spirit and the fruit of the Spirit (Acts 6:1-7).

4. *Motivated.* Care Group leaders need to be enthused about their faith and the possibilities of their group. They have a

clear vision and relationship that guides them in willing service (1 Pet. 5: 1-7).

5. *Grounded.* Christian leaders need to be grounded in Scripture and clearly committed to Christ and to Christ's body—the church. They need to teach the way of Jesus and guard against false doctrine (Acts 20:27-32).

To be chosen and commissioned to serve as a Care Group leader, you will generally need:

1. To have the above qualities
2. To be trained in the arts of listening and dialogue
3. To be committed to supervision and continuing education
4. To be committed to the sponsoring church's membership, purposes, and philosophy of ministry

Accept the Responsibility

Together with your pastor you will be responsible for the pastoral care of the members in your Care Group. It is an exciting responsibility! Don't shrink from it.

More and more pastors are encouraging lay ministry. Given the opportunity, more and more lay people like you are investing time and energy into learning the skills required to do competent ministry. Carl F. George of the Fuller Institute observes that "laity will take ministry to a small-size group so seriously that they will prefer such ministry to the recognition of elected office." [48]

Together with your pastor you will want to agree on a job description. The following might serve as a model.

Care Group Leader Job Description

Purpose

A Care Group leaders mission is to provide caring, servant leadership and ministry to the persons in a group so they concretely experience the acceptance, forgiveness, and fullness of life in Christ and in Christian community.

Accountability

Each Care Group leader is directly accountable to the pastor (or the small group coordinator). The pastor, in turn, is accountable for this ministry through the church council/board to the congregation.

Responsibilities: A Care Group Leader is responsible

1. For forming a group by recruiting three to twelve persons including an apprentice. (Some leaders may be asked to lead groups that have been formed in other ways.)

2. For the effective pastoral care of the persons in the group (together with the pastor).

3. For modeling Christian discipleship and maintaining his or her personal, spiritual life through regular Bible reading, prayer, and personal discipline.

4. Details of responsibility will include:

- Fostering a climate of acceptance and mutual care in the group.
- Helping the group to agree on a covenant which will include the purpose of the group, meeting time, and materials to be used.
- Delegating to individual members of the group such responsibilities as hosting, leading music, occasionally leading the study, planning a retreat, and exploring service projects.
- Leading the group in dialogue so each member is free to contribute thoughts and feelings.
- Timing the group meetings so there is an effective and balanced emphasis on fellowship, Bible study, sharing, and mission.
- Helping train an apprentice to become capable of leading either the original group or a new group.
- Ministering to the individual members of the group as needed.
- Referring to the pastor or a trained counselor members in need of professional care and counseling.
- Encouraging regular church attendance by each member.
- Attending monthly meetings of the Care Group leaders for the purpose of peer supervision and continuing education.

Choose Your Leadership Style and Pattern

Each of us develops our own leadership style. Some styles are more helpful than others and may require us to change how we lead. The four most common styles of leadership are domineering, authoritarian, democratic, and laissez-faire. Which is your usual style?

1. Domineering: Domineering or autocratic leaders control the agenda and dynamics of a group. They determine a group's goals, policies, and content. Domineering leaders usually talk too much and focus attention on themselves, which may make members resentful, hostile, and frustrated. This is not an appropriate leadership style for a Care Group.

2. Authoritative: Authoritative leaders are definite yet responsive. They make suggestions and give guidance but also actively invite member input in the process of choosing goals, policies, and content. They take responsibility until others can assume it and use personal power to empower others. This style of leadership is helpful in the beginning stages of a group's life. As the group matures, flexibility and sensitivity become imperative.

3. Democratic: Democratic leaders share control, leadership, and responsibility with group members. They believe in other people as equal partners and may invite them to lead group meetings. They may work themselves out of a job as they are challenged to new assignments. This is the most appropriate leadership style for most Care Groups.

4. Laissez-Faire: Laissez-faire or permissive leaders may allow a group to drift with little guidance. They permit members to lead according to interests or abilities without regulating or applying controls. One member may monopolize the time while others begin backing away from or fragmenting the group due to lack of direction or achievement. This type of leadership is discouraged in Care Groups.

There are a variety of leadership patterns which you and your group may wish to consider as you think of how you wish to conduct your meetings. Roberta Hestenes outlines them as follows:[49]

1. The same leader each week. This is the most common pattern for support, evangelism, and mission groups and is also an acceptable pattern for nurture groups. The advantage of having the same leader each week is continuity, a familiar pattern, and the likelihood of development in the depth of the group as the weeks go by, because members feel secure knowing how the leader will lead the group.

2. Partnership. In this method, two or three people are designated as group leaders. They share the various tasks of leadership week by week. One member may lead one week and another person the next time. Or according to their gifts and interests, one member may lead one part of the meeting and another a different part.

3. Rotating leadership. In this pattern, each member takes a turn at leading. The advantage is that no one person is burdened with preparation for all of the group meetings and all have an opportunity to learn by leading. The disadvantage is that some may not be clear what leading a group really involves. Also, the ongoing pastoral needs of group members may not be attended to.

There is no such thing as a leaderless group. If a group does not decide on a leadership pattern suitable to its situation, it cannot expect to function productively. Don't be afraid of strong democratic leaders. Good leaders make for good groups.

Lead a Dialogue

The lead pastors key task may be to preach and the teachers to teach but your most important task as a Care Group leader is to lead a dialogue! Albert Wollen persuasively argues that the greatest need of a small group leader is to "discover how to use dialogue effectively." [50]

Leading Care Group meetings in good dialogue fashion

week after week is a rewarding challenge. In the group you will dialogue about your group's purpose, projects, and goals. You will discuss the meaning and application of Scripture passages. You may even dialogue with God in prayer.

You may also want to have individual dialogues outside of group time about members' personal goals, projects, and life purposes. You may be called on to interact with them concerning their gifts, problems, and relationships. Don't be afraid to interact with them in prayer.

Lyman Coleman says that a small group leader "is not necessarily a teacher, biblical scholar, strong or most popular personality, movie star, dictator, psychologist, extrovert, elder, or wise sage. A small group leader is someone committed to being aware of and managing the process of the group toward the goals the group has set." [51]

Leadership and ministry are not easy. But you will experience many satisfactions. These come in developing close relationships, in seeing members grow in their Christian life, in overcoming problems, and in seeing members go on to minister in new ways.

For further study in the art of leading a group, consult the next three chapters. Also of help are John Mallison's excellent book, *Building Small Groups in the Christian Community*, (West Ryde, Australia, Renewal Publications, 1978), and *Good Things Come in Small Groups*, written by a small group (Downers Grove, Ill.: InterVarsity Press, 1985).

Leadership

An Application Exercise

Where on this continuum would you place your leader's style?

Autocratic   Authoritarian   Democratic   Laissez-Faire

/ ——————— / ——————— / ——————— /

Determines goals	Identifies goals	Lacks goals
Controls discussion	Leads a dialogue	Lets strongest lead
Focuses on self	Focuses on gifts	Focuses on freedom
Prompts reaction	Prompts harmony	Prompts individualism

Give your leader friendly feedback on leadership functions performed in today's meeting. Indicate true (T) or false (F) for each of the following statements. Add comments.

Our leader: He/she did it by:
T/F

_____ Showed personal care.   _____

_____ Listened.   _____

_____ Kept the group's goals in focus.   _____

_____ Prompted dialogue between us.   _____

_____ Utilized our gifts.   _____

_____ Led the group to decision.   _____

_____ Counseled and encouraged us.   _____

Think whom to invite into your group. Finish these sentences.

1. I would like to start a (check one):
   _____ nurture care group
   _____ support care group
   _____ evangelistic care group
   _____ mission care group
2. For an apprentice or coleader I would like to invite. . . .
3. Three other people I would like to invite are. . . .

11 Group Participation

Get All Members Involved

An important goal for a Care Group leader is to have everyone in the group involved. Not all will participate equally on a verbal level, but everyone needs a sense of ownership in the group. Steve Barker of InterVarsity says, "One of your key concerns should be, 'How can I help others feel that the group is not "my group" but "our group"?' " [52]

Research indicates that after thirty days people remember 10 percent of what they hear, 50 percent of what they see, 70 percent of what they say and 90 percent of what they do. [53] The challenge is to invite group members to share with each other what they are discovering and then do it. The goal of a Care Group is to go beyond learning to showing care.

Participation diminishes as a group grows. Seven to nine members is ideal. When a group reaches ten, it should commission two or three of its members together with your apprentice, to begin a new group.

Lyman Coleman suggests that when a group becomes larger than seven, the Bible study should be done in groups of four. He calls this the "fearsome foursome," because in groups of four, people are neither afraid to speak nor to take leadership. If you use the "fearsome four" principle, the agenda will look like this.

Gathering time (15 minutes): While the group is arriving, serve refreshments and start off with icebreakers, songs, prayer, etc.

Bible study/sharing (30 minutes): For this brief time when you need maximum participation, divide into groups of three or four (four at the dining table, three at the kitchen table, four downstairs in the family room, etc.)

Ask someone in each group to be the discussion leader and follow the agenda of questions. In groups of four, everyone can participate and you can finish the Bible study in 30 minutes. Be back for the real purpose of the group with plenty of time for caring.

Caring time (30-45 minutes): All back together, the group moves to the real purpose of the group—to care for one another. There is plenty of time for this because you did not get bogged down in the Bible study discussion. The caring time starts off with songs of prayer and praise and sharing of prayer requests.[54]

As leader you should ask for feedback from time to time on what might improve full participation. Is it the way you sit? The materials? The way you ask questions? Some dynamic in the group? A critical climate and an over talkative leader or group member are the two greatest inhibitors of participation.

Discuss Through Dialogue

Preaching and lecturing are efficient means of one-way communication. These forms are helpful for purposes of inspiration and transmitting knowledge, but a Care Group is not the place to preach and lecture. To ensure good dialogue, a Care Group leader should aim to do less than half of the talking!

Teaching is usually a combination of lecture and discussion. Often it is characterized by questions and answers. The leader is seen as the expert with the answers. Sometimes he or she becomes an oral examiner. The emphasis is on teaching and learning. Care Group leaders need to aim for more dialogue than happens in the usual Sunday school or seminar class.

Laissez-faire leadership often leads to cozy dialogues between pairs of members or allows for a "junior lecturer" to dominate. Freedom to participate should characterize a Care Group but the leader needs to maintain control of the process and direction so everyone has opportunity to participate toward a worthy goal.

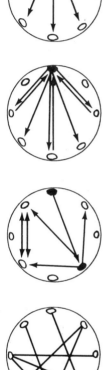

A leader of dialogue will place the emphasis on speaking the truth in love and receiving feedback, which should happen not only between the leader and group members but also among members of the group. Care Groups should be characterized by lots of back and forth dialogue among members.

Jesus used dialogue. He would tell a parable or make a statement, then ask for feedback. On many occasions the disciples discussed principles among themselves, then explored them further with Jesus. The apostle Paul also used dialogue. At Mars Hill he made a basic point, then entered into vigorous dialogue (see Matt. 12:46-50; 13:10, Acts 17:17).

Dialogue is the missing ingredient in many churches!

Churches are stereotyped as being places of one-way communication. The larger the congregation, the less interaction there is among attenders unless there is some form of small group life. Bruce Larson says, "We do not know of a single church now producing live lay people which does not have at its heart some form of small group fellowship." [55]

Learn to Model and Lead Dialogue

Five steps will help you lead a good dialogue.

1. Attend to your members and help them to attend to each other. When you speak, look at the person you are addressing. Establish eye contact. Lean forward slightly and listen actively. Such actions show you care. They show you are ready to accept the other as an equal. When members slouch down or over-relax while speaking, invite them repeat what they just said. Their comment was important. To recognize that importance, ask them to repeat the comment while you make eye contact and lean forward. As leader, you need to set the pace for this kind of attending.

2. Restate in your own words what another speaker has said. Confirm that you have heard and understood what a speaker was actually trying to say. Go for understanding! Feel free to say, "I understand you're saying . . ." or "feeling. . . ."

3. Use "I" instead of "you" messages. Communication in your group will improve when each member takes responsibility for ideas and feelings by saying "I." To say " I feel . . ." or "I think . . ." is much more direct and helpful than "Some people think . . ." or "Some people believe. . . ." Draw participants into deeper dialogue by saying, "I would like to know more about that," or, "Then what happened?" or "So what difference did it make?"

4. Redirect questions to the group. Especially if you are often asked the questions, turn to a member and say, "I'd be interested in what Jo has to say about that." Redirecting, with

use of names, encourages members to talk with each other, not just back and forth with you.

5. Summarize and move on. When a point has been made and adequately responded to, summarize what has been learned, add your own insight, and move to the next question. Dialogue must be kept on track.

Continue to Increase Participation

Following are several additional, well-tested tips for increasing participation.

1. Encourage participation by asking several members to contribute answers to a single question. "What do the rest of you think?" or "Is there anything else which could be added?" are ways of encouraging participation.

2. Never answer your own question. Either use an alternate question or move to another area for discussion. Do not be afraid of pauses or silent time. Your members need time to think about a question or response.

3. Call on hesitant members or give them an encouraging nod. Note by facial expression or body posture when a member has something to say. The extroverted members in your group will often offer information before you ask, while you need to "ask it out" of introverts.

4. Receive all contributions warmly. Affirm members for their participation. Never bluntly reject what someone says. If you think the information is incorrect, ask in a friendly manner, "Is that actually what it says?" or "What do some of the rest of you think?"

5. Restrain an over-talkative member. Sit directly beside a talker. Switch your gaze to a silent member. The talker may begin addressing that person.

You may need to speak privately to over-talkative members. Share your goals for participation from all members. Enlist talkers in encouraging all to participate. Gently point out what over-participation is doing to the group.

Discern the Gifts and Roles

Each member in a group has a gift and is a potential leader in that area of giftedness. The ideal is for everyone's gift to be discerned and affirmed for use in the group, church, and world. You may want to do a gifts discernment questionnaire which will help you to know each person at a deeper level.

Each person in a group plays a role. Some members may be steered towards playing more helpful roles. In her *Small Groups Leader Training Course,* Judy Hamlin says, "Always be on the look-out for a gifted person. For instance, call on a natural singer to lead singing, or ask if anyone will serve as worship leader for the group. Continue this process until you have appointed all to positions of leadership. Some members may have more unusual talents. If you have an amateur photographer, let him serve as your small-group photographer, and create a scrapbook. Be flexible. Don't be confined by job descriptions." [56]

Following are roles often carried by members of a group.

- *Host or hostess*: Helps members feel welcome and comfortable. Arranges the room, materials, or refreshments.
- *Teacher*: Leads in giving input and receiving feedback. Does research and preparation in advance.
- *Pastor*: Discerns members' emotional and spiritual needs. May ask, "How can I pray for you this week?"
- *Spiritual director*: Helps members achieve their highest level of discipline or spiritual development.
- *Evangelist*: Invites group members to make a decision or to invite new people to the fellowship.
- *Activist*: Organizes a project, takes action, or helps group members take action or organize a project.
- *Encourager*: Brings others into the discussion and encourages their contribution.

- *Clarifier*: Steps in when confusion and conflict occur. Defines the problems concisely and points out the issues.
- *Proposer*: Fits together the pieces of a dialogue and proposes a direction or a needed action.

Keep an Open Climate

Participation happens when there is an open climate. Group members need to feel accepted from the moment they arrive. Begin with an open sharing question. Invite their ideas and feelings throughout the meeting. The dynamics of the first meeting will often set the pace for participation.

Interrupt business as usual if someone has a special joy or burden. This is called "immediacy." Be immediately ready to focus full and sensitive attention on a vital concern. If necessary, scrap the prepared agenda.

Nurture honesty. Recognize that any good in our lives is to God's credit, not our own. This recognition will help you affirm the good in each others' lives while avoiding a spirit of bragging. Honesty about your own weakness and God's good grace contributes to a warm, genuine climate into which you can bring nonchurched friends.

For further study of dialogue read Albert Wollen, *Miracles Happen in Group Bible Study* (Glendale, Calif., Regal Books, 1976).

Participation
An Application Exercise[57]

What were the patterns of participation in today's group meeting? Ask a member to keep a record according to the following guidelines.

1. In the space below, draw a circle (as modeled) for each member of your group as he or she is seated.
2. The first time someone speaks, draw an arrow from that person's circle. If he speaks to the group as a whole, draw the arrow into the center (A). If she speaks to a particular person, draw the arrow to that circle (B). Each subsequent time a person speaks, draw a bar through the arrow line (C). Note that (C) has spoken three times. If someone speaks a long time, you may wish to draw a bar for each minute and an arch to show that it was a long speech (D). If someone asks a question, you may want to put a question mark beside the bar (E).

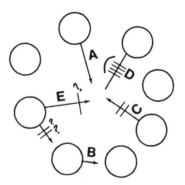

3. What did your leader do to draw out silent members? Restrain over-talkers? Enhance dialogue between you?
4. What can your group or leader do to improve participation and interaction at next week's meeting?

Report to each other your plans for beginning a group. See last week's evaluation.

12 Creativity and Conflict

Encourage Creativity

Everyone is creative. Our Creator saw to that. Each is unique and has a free will to both develop and exercise uniqueness. When creativity dies, something crucial ceases to be. One purpose of a Care Group is to make the most of all persons' creativity—to build on their gifts and strengths.

The abilities of creative people are almost limitless. This is especially true when abilities are joined in complementary ways. Jesus made the astonishing statements that "if two of you on earth agree about anything you ask for, it will be done for you by my Father in heaven" (Matt. 18:19) and "anyone who has faith in me will do what I have been doing. He will do even greater things than these" (John 14:12).

Recognize that Conflict Is Inevitable

Whenever creative people come together, conflicts will occur. It is impossible to live without conflict. Even among Christian groups the issue is not *if* conflict will occur but *how* it will be managed. During his ministry, Jesus had many conflicts with people and there were numerous conflicts within his group of twelve. We can be sure of the same!

Leaders, in a special way, experience conflict. Often they are in the center of it. Paul Miller observes that "groups tend to be conservative. Society makes most of its progress because of the innovators, but it gives them a rough time." [58]

In our world conflicts are generally viewed as something to either hide from or win. In a Care Group you are challenged to see conflicts as opportunities for growth.

Without conflict we would become set in our ways and not change. When someone wants to do something different, there is potential for conflict but also potential for change. Conflicts provide opportunities to discuss differences, learn from them, and seek an agreeable consensus which will likely leave those involved at a different place than when they began.

David and Frank Johnson observe that "if differences are avoided instead of openly expressed, hidden conflicts will persist. The cost to the group will be greater than if they are openly confronted and properly reconciled." They challenge any two people or groups "to openly face and to quickly reconcile the conflicts as they emerge." [59]

Identify the Sources of Conflict

There are four common sources of conflict.

1. Conflicts related to goals. Everyone has goals. Goals help us plan our directions and look forward to new possibilities. Goals help us work together with others who have similar goals. Goals also provide a basis for measuring our progress.

But when two people or groups of people have differing goals, the potential for conflict exists. When goals conflict, decisions need to be made concerning which goals to pursue and which to drop or alter. Creativity and growth come when all goals are studied and the reasons behind all are understood.

Every person and group has both relational and achievement goals. When they conflict, we may be forced to ask, "Do I maintain my relational goals and give up my achievement goals or do I go for achievement and sacrifice relationship?"

Careful dialogue is needed to understand how deeply held and important are the achievement and the relational goals. How much pain will be experienced in giving up one goal or the other? Good dialogue can increase the quality and depth of a relationship by bringing deeper understanding. Good dialogue can also rally a person toward an achievement. Creativity is released for action when relational and achievement goals are brought together.

2. Conflicts related to controls. A group will normally experience some conflict over leadership and control. As leader of a Care Group, be prepared to reconcile perceptions and feelings related to your control or lack of it. Guard against becoming defensive.

Several stages in group life can be anticipated. Each stage of change has its potential for conflict or misunderstanding.

a. Usually a group will begin with considerable dependence on its leader. The leader controls the group's schedule and leads communication by nature of the role. Many groups stay at this level, which we might call level one. "It's Jim's group," members say. This inhibits creativity and growth.

b. As members become willing and able to assume leadership, resistance to your leadership or even competition for it can be expected. A wise leader will seek to delegate aspects of leadership to members. This will help the group come to level two, the "this is our group" stage.

c. As your group takes ownership for itself, new ideas and directions will emerge. As leader you must now learn to assume the role of cheerleader even while continuing to formulate basic policy. Your group will hopefully become inter-dependent. You and your members will arrive at level three realizing that "this is our group and we need each other."

For interdependence to happen, you need to help your

group build on the gifts of all. A fully involved group is a life-giving, creative one in which conflicts are being properly managed. If your group reaches this stage, be thankful!

3. Conflicts related to personality. Each of us is different from another in a thousand ways. Each difference has the potential for being a gift or a conflict. Group members will differ from each other in perceptions, roles, goals, values, and personality types. Basic understanding of differences will help group members accept each other and even to appreciate the strengths and uniquenesses each brings.

In some situations it might be helpful to have the group take the Meyers-Briggs or some similar personality-type test. The Meyers-Briggs test, with many good interpretations, can be found in *Please Understand Me*, by David Keirsey and Marilyn Bates.[60]

4. Conflicts related to sin and disobedience. Some but not all conflicts are the result of sin. Conflicts related to goals, controls, and personality can be honest differences without being contrary to God's will. However, sin is the major cause of destructive conflict in our world. When we have and pursue differences in thought, attitude, or action that are contrary to the moral laws of God, there is conflict with God and each other. Confession of sin is taking an honest look at the situation and making basic choices in relation to what is causing the conflict. Asking forgiveness is God's way of reconciling sin.

Making confession and asking forgiveness will happen often in a healthy group. When an offending person recognizes a problem, a good way to bring reconciliation is simply to say, "I realize how much what I [said, thought, or did] hurt you. I want to ask, 'Will you forgive me?' "

Deal with the Conflict Immediately

There are four common ways of dealing with conflict. The fourth is most helpful.

1. Avoidance. Leaders and members of groups tend to stay clear of any topic or person that will stir dissent. In one way or another, they withdraw from the issue, person, or group.

Avoiding differences may be wise when the issues are trivial and counting to ten is advisable when you are ready to explode! But generally avoidance and delay keep group members from getting close to each other. In Ephesians 4, Paul says "In your anger do not sin." He goes on to urge, "Don't let the sun go down while you are still angry" (v. 26). In other words, face and resolve the differences before the evening ends. Don't avoid them!

2. Giving in . . . losing. Christians with a service mentality sometimes feel that giving up their wants and rights is the only way to group harmony. They believe they are called to sacrifice and suffer. But sometimes "giving in" means "giving up" a creative action or a correct viewpoint. What if that action or viewpoint is closest to the will of God?

Each member of your group has equal rights. Some feelings and issues should be pursued. There is a place for proper assertiveness. At first it might cause conflict, but it may be the way to creativity and harmony. Proper assertiveness should not be confused with aggressive behavior, just as giving in should not be confused with humility. Proper assertiveness stands firm for an action or point of view without violating the rights of others. When appropriate, help your members articulate a point of view or stand firm in relationship to it.

3. Competing—winning. Some people revel in competition. They have a compulsive need to win an argument just for the sake of winning. They want to be on top just for the sake of having power.

There is a place for assertiveness and there are times in life when we have to be willing to go to the mat for what we believe. But using power to overcome opposition does not resolve it. It merely drives it underground where it festers and often gains destructive momentum. Avoid getting into win-lose situations!

4. Carefronting. David Augsburger, in *Caring Enough to Confront*,[61] coined the term "carefronting" to combine loving care for another person with an honest confronting of the differences that separate people or groups. Carefronting is a problem-solving mode that takes time and emotional energy. It seeks to find a position in which all members retain strong relationships with each other while reaching an acceptable goal.

A key rule for resolving conflict is that *all points of view must be clearly heard and understood.* When people and values are heard, a negotiated settlement is usually possible. A negotiated settlement is usually better than a win.

Follow Tested Mediation Steps

Following are six tested steps to use in reconciling conflict.

a. Name the issues or differences. Be quick to identify and name differences of your members in regard to goals, control, values, or personality. Report to the group that a conflict exists. Carefront it early when it is small.

b. Identify the key issue to be worked on. If there are several issues and differences, decide which is most important and begin with it. Have all parties involved at the meeting. If only some in your group are involved in the conflict, meet at a time when only they will be there. Begin with prayer.

c. Have representatives of the different points of view describe the points of view clearly. **Make sure all points of view have been clearly heard and understood.** Help members clarify by asking, "What do you mean? Could you restate that?"

d. Have representatives describe the feelings and possible consequences involved. It often helps to have an opponent of a point of view express how he or she feels the other person is feeling about the issue. As mediator, show care for the anxiety, fear, anger, or whatever emotion is being experienced before addressing the details of the issue.

e. Brainstorm possible solutions without evaluating them. When solutions have been listed, evaluate pros and cons of the most likely ones. Explore them until you have reached consensus or the best negotiated settlement possible. You may have to carefront and be assertive to arrive at a solution that fully respects both or all points of view.

f. Write and announce the resolution to those involved or affected.

Face Other Problems with Courage

Problem solving is not an interruption of our work. It *is* our work! We have been given the ministry of reconciliation (2 Cor. 5:18). Be confident that in Christ there is a solution to every problem. Following are five problems that are common in groups.

1. A critical or antagonistic member. Listen carefully to that member. Try to find the good in the member's comments. Don't get defensive or let the group get tense and excited. Visit with the person one-on-one to find out if there is a personal problem. If a member is a true antagonist, you will need to ask the person to leave the group until cured of the illness that creates negativity in nearly all situations. Such a person will destroy the group.[62]

2. Breach of confidentiality. Carefront the member privately. Clarify how breaking confidentiality destroys trust. Only safe and public things will be discussed in a group where there is no assurance of confidentiality. Lack of confidentiality will not allow your group to function as a true Christian community. Have the member confess the breach of confidentiality to the individual offended and recommit yourselves as a group to not sharing even with close friends or spouses unless explicit permission is given by the person sharing.

3. Aimlessness or apathy. If interest has declined or attendance has fallen off, stop business as usual and renegotiate your covenant. Rediscover what are the real needs of the group members. Has a key component—acceptance, study, sharing, or mission been neglected?

4. Exclusive attitude. When a group has not grown for several months, it may justify itself by saying that newcomers would destroy the closeness of the group. Review the "empty chair" policy of the church's Care Group program. This policy can be that at every meeting (or at an agreed on time) an empty chair will be pulled into the circle and the group asked to pray for someone to fill the chair at the next meeting. When the group reaches nine, the group automatically multiplies either in the home where it is meeting or by launching a new group.

5. Group burn-out. Sometimes groups stay together too long. Members either feel obligated to come to another meeting or they become a mere social entity. Recognize that there are usually two purposes for Care Groups—(1) to care for the people you now have, and (2) to reach the people you don't have. Hold a graduation party and encourage members to parent new groups or to join groups where they can meet new people and new challenges.

To further explore the matter of conflict resolution read *Caring Enough to Confront* by David Augsburger (Ventura, Calif.: Regal Books, 1980); *Joining Together,* by Johnson and Johnson (Englewood Cliffs, N.Y.: Prentice-Hall, Inc., 1982); and *Repairing the Breach*, by Ronald S. Kraybill (Scottdale, Pa.: Herald Press, 1981).

Conflict Resolution
An Application Exercise

Identify a conflict that emerged in today's meeting or a conflict that you feel exists between the group and your leader. In what way did you deal with it?

_____**Avoidance**—We showed little concern for either the *issue* or the *relationships* involved. We wanted the issue to go away or the person to get out.

_____**Giving in**—We didn't care much about getting our way or standing for the right. We lost the battle on the issue to save our *relationships.*

_____**Competing**—We were very concerned about the *issue* and wanted to win. We didn't care much about what it meant to relationships.

_____**Carefronting**—We were concerned about *both* the issue and the relationships involved. We were not willing to sacrifice either and tried to negotiate a solution.

What do you feel should be done about the conflict? Is it resolved? If not, which of the following steps will help lead to resolution? (Check as many as apply.)

_____1. Name the issues or differences.
_____2. Identify the key issue.
_____3. Describe each point of view.
_____4. Describe the feelings and consequences of each.
_____5. Brainstorm possible solutions.
_____6. Write and announce the resolution.

13 Supervision and Continuing Education

Welcome Regular Supervision

Supervision is the key to offering quality Christian care and leadership to your Care Group members. Supervision is not to be confused with some forms of dictatorial shepherding in which an authority places requirements on you, then demands strict obedience. A good supervisor helps the person supervised to explore options, then lets the supervisee make the final decision on what to do.

Supervision is a supportive relationship between you and your pastor or small group coordinator. You will also have a supportive relationship with Care Group peers, with whom you will exchange supervision as both giver and receiver. The goal is to improve the quality of ministry being offered in your church.

Because supervision is key, it is a requirement in the Care Group ministry. A Care Group whose leader or facilitator is not in supervision should not be listed as a group sponsored by the church.

Supervision is set up to be an encouraging, rewarding experience. Satisfaction comes from doing a job well. It also comes from having close relationships with others who can identify with your thoughts, feelings, and experiences. Satisfaction comes when you know you are being cared for with the same quality of care you are seeking to give.

You and your supervisor will meet once a month, possibly more. Look forward to these times of fellowship, sharing, prayer, and continuing education!

Work Closely with Your Pastor

Your pastor, or a coordinator of small groups, will be director of the Care Group Ministry program. In that capacity he or she will be a pastor to you and perhaps a cheerleader. Support may be given both personally and from the pulpit. It is to your advantage to nurture a close working relationship with your pastor. Don't be afraid to call him or her often or to stop in at the office when you have a question or concern. Just as Jesus gave more time to his twelve disciples than to all the rest of the people in the world put together, so your pastor wants to spend special time with you.

The relationship of pastor to Care Group leaders might be diagramed as follows:

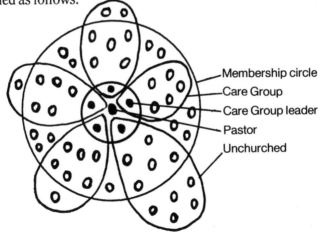

Membership circle
Care Group
Care Group leader
Pastor
Unchurched

Meet Monthly with Your Peers

Each month, and possibly twice a month, your pastor will convene Care Group leaders for a full evening. You will check in with each other, experience in-depth supervision, and explore continuing education topics. Your schedule will look something as follows:

Opening	5 minutes
Peer supervision (in groups of 5 to 8)	55 minutes
Break	15 minutes
Continuing education	40 minutes
Closing	5 minutes

There will be three parts to the fifty-five-minute Peer Supervision period.

1. An overall view. As you arrive, you will lend your Weekly Care Group Record Sheet to your pastor (see Appendix B). A quick glance will remind your pastor who is in your group. It will also inform the pastor of how often your group has met and how you are evaluating your experiences together. The pastor will return the sheet to you later in the evening.

2. A one-minute check-in statement. The first ten minutes of your time together will be given to hearing brief check-in statements from each of the five to eight Care Group leaders in your supervisory group. They will be brief, honest statements taken from your Monthly Leader's Check-in Sheet which you will have prepared in advance (see Appendix C).

Your pastor, or peer group facilitator (if your church has more than eight groups), will make a brief response. If you are having a special problem, the pastor may choose it for problem solving. About ten minutes will be given at each meeting to help one of you solve a special problem.

3. In-depth evaluation of ministry. The main part (thirty minutes) of your supervision session will go to helping one Care Group leader evaluate and improve his or her ministry.

Each of you will get a turn—one each meeting. When it is your turn, you will give a five- to eight-minute report in regard to your ministry. The report will be based on material from the In-depth Ministry Assessment Form (Appendix D), which you will have filled out. Your supervision group will agree on a focus question from Appendix E to help explore your ministry at a deeper level than allowed for by the brief monthly check-in reports, based on Appendix C.

This thirty-minute time together with your peers will help you explore your feelings, thoughts, and processes in regard to serving as a leader and lay pastor. The group will be supportive and seek to help you discover the most effective ways of giving care and leadership to your group.

Welcome Continuing Education

A key to motivation is learning skills and having the opportunity and responsibility to use them. This is what continuing education is about. It will help you develop new skills and improve existing skills. Continuing education topics will focus on challenges and issues you will face in your role as a Care Group leader.

Appendix F lists fifteen possible continuing education topics. You will be invited to add to this list, then prioritize which you feel are the most important. Together with other Care Group leaders, you will explore the topics one at a time.

In continuing education you will spend about half of the time, twenty minutes, in listening to a presentation and the other half in discussing the topic. Your pastor or coordinator will either make the presentation or ask a resource person to assist. For discussion you may either want to stay together, break into groups of four, or go back to your supervision groups of five to eight. You decide.

As you keep developing your understandings and skills in leadership and ministry, you will experience satisfaction and a sense of well-being. There is joy in personal growth and in doing a job to the best of your expanding abilities!

Keep Your Purpose Clear

As we conclude this manual, we must return to the beginning. What is the vision God is giving you for small groups? What is the purpose for having and leading a small group? Reasons include:

- to care for each other
- to pray with and for each other
- to be available in time of need
- to stimulate spiritual growth
- to invite and integrate new people
- to experience deeper relationships
- to respond to God's call in the world.

You need to keep the purpose of your leadership role clear. You have been called to meet the needs of those looking to you for ministry and leadership. Your own needs will be secondary.

The challenge of being a lay pastor to a small number of persons is not small. If you try it, you need to be warmly affirmed! You will receive your ultimate affirmation from God, who will say "Well done, good and faithful servant! You have been faithful with a few things; I will put you in charge of many things. Come and share your master's happiness" (Matt. 25:21).

When things do not go well, know that God understands. In Jesus Christ he led a difficult group of twelve. He will know how you feel!

May the Spirit dwell in you richly, filling you with joy and peace and courage for the endeavor to which God is calling you!

Your Small Group Dream
An Application Exercise

How will you put into practice the training received in this manual? Write answers to the following six questions and share them with your group and then with your pastor.

1. If you could start a Care Group, what kind of a group would you start?

_____ nurture/Bible study/covenant group

_____ special support/recovery group

_____ evangelistic group

_____ mission group

2. Who would be your target group, those most likely to respond?

3. What would be the group's specific purpose? What would the group seek to achieve?

4. If you could have your wish, whom would you want as co-leader?

5. Who would be the first three people you would like to invite to be in this group?

6. What would you like to choose for your curriculum?

APPENDIX A

Group Member Ministry Report
For Care Group Members

It is your turn to report on your ministry. Before coming to the next Care Group meeting, write one or two sentence answers to each of the following questions. Be prepared to briefly share your answers with the group during the sharing and prayer time. If your calling or the focus of your ministry is not clear, let your Care Group help discern your gifts and possible opportunities.

As you report, focus on the way you are ministering. Do not mention the names of people to whom you are relating. Rather seek help for how you can better work with a certain type of problem. For example say, "I am working with a twelve-year-old as a Big Brother. I am seeking to help him be open in communication and clear in his directions. I like the fellow and he likes me but the problem is that his mother is attracted to me. This Care Group could help me know how I might relate to her."

1. Describe the nature of your ministry.

2. What are your current goals for your ministry?

3. What is going well in your ministry and what is not going well?

4. How can this Care Group help you in your ministry?

5. How can we pray for you?

APPENDIX B

Care Group Record Sheet
For Care Group Leaders

Update this Care Group Record Sheet after each meeting. Hand it to your pastor or supervisory group leader as you enter your monthly meeting with other group leaders. He or she will look it over briefly and hand it back to you after you make your check-in report.

Regular Members   Irregular Members

_____   _____   _____

_____   _____   _____

_____   _____   _____

_____   _____   _____

_____   _____   _____

Dates of Mtgs	Atten- dance	No. of Guests	Evaluate your experiences 1=poor; 5=excellent				Comments
			Fellow- ship	Study	Prayer	Mission	

APPENDIX C

Monthly Leader's Check-in Sheet
For Care Group Leaders

Before coming to a Care Group leaders' meeting, write brief answers to each of the following questions. Briefly share your answers at the beginning of the meeting during check-in time.

1. Describe the nature of your group and what it is doing.

2. What do the group members need and what are they getting from you and the group experience?

3. What are your current goals for ministry with the group?

4. What is going well in your Care Group and what is not?

5. How can this supervision group help you be a better leader-minister to your group?

In-depth Ministry Assessment Form
For Care Group Leaders

The purpose of an in-depth assessment is to help you reflect and focus on the ministry you are doing with your Care Group. It will assist you in providing pertinent information about your caring relationships so your peers can help you in your ministry and you in theirs. This form can be an outline for your presentation to the group.

Be as complete as possible in your assessment. Protect confidentiality when deciding what to report. As you prepare your report, concentrate most of all on the caring relationship that exists between you and your group. Secondarily focus on your feelings and skills. Try to avoid talking about the situations and problems of your group members. Never mention names of persons involved unless this is public knowledge and will help improve your work as group leader.

1. Approximate number of weeks or months the group has been together. _____

2. Pattern of meetings and relationships.
     _____ We have met at least weekly since we began.
     _____ We started out meeting weekly but meetings have become less frequent.
     _____ I have met individually with _____ of the group members.
     _____ Group members are involved in prayer partner arrangements.

3. What is your relationship to the pastor or overall coordinator? How has it been helpful?

4. Who else is ministering to the members of your group?

_____ Pastor   _____ Medical personnel
_____ Teachers   _____ Sunday school teacher
_____ Social workers   _____ Churches
_____ Other _____   _____ Other _____

5. In one paragraph, describe the identified need which brought you and the group together. Is the need still pressing?

6. In one or two sentences, state the goals you have for ministry to this group and its members.

7. In one paragraph, summarize the approach you have been taking to minister to the persons in this group.

8. Assessment of the caring relationship—

    a. How do you feel about your relationship with the group members?

    b. What has been the nature of the group's response to your ministry?

    c. What do you think has been going well in your relationship?

    d. What has been challenging, frustrating, or problematic?

    e. What do you see as the future direction of your ministry in regard to this group?

9. With questions, concerns, issues, or areas of need do you want your peers in the supervision group to help you?

10. What focus question or set of questions might the supervision group use in discussing your caring relationship?

APPENDIX E

Focus Questions
For Peer Group Supervision

Choose the set of questions and the question that will help assess and develop the presenting person's ministry. What will get at the crucial issue or situation?

A. Focus on the relationship between the group leader and group

1. Describe the relationship between you and the group.
   a. What are the strongest and most rewarding aspects?
   b. What aspects most need improvement?
2. Do either you or your group get frustrated because of inappropriate expectations?
   a. Expectations that you place on the group or yourself.
   b. Expectations group members place on you or themselves.
   c. How are these expectations communicated?
3. Is your focus on process or results?
   a. How often do you offer solutions, give advice, or rescue group members?
   b. In what ways do you pressure yourself to make things happen?
   c. In what ways do you pressure group members to change their thinking or behavior?

B. Focus on spiritual concerns

1. What faith issues (purpose to life, sin, salvation, justice) seem important to you? To your group members?
2. How would you like to see God's presence become more real in your relationships to the group?
   a. Have you encountered Jesus in your group members? How?
   b. Have your group members encountered Jesus in you? How?

3. How appropriate and effective are your use of traditional Christian resources?
    a. How do you use the Bible?
    b. How do you experience prayer?
    c. How do you bestow a blessing upon your group members?

C. Focus on the feelings, skills, and role of the leader

1. Do the values, beliefs, or mannerisms of your group frustrate you?
    a. Do you own responsibility for your feelings toward the group?
    b. Are you able to express appropriately your feelings to the group? To us?
    c. How are your feelings helping or hindering your ministry to the group?
2. How are you doing as a Care Group leader?
    a. How well are you able to listen? Give examples.
    b. How well are you able to facilitate dialogue?
    c. How assertive are you with your group? Give examples.

D. Focus on problems in the group

1. What are your group members problems as you see them? What do they think the problems are?
2. Do any aspects of your group members' situations seem too great for you to handle? If so, which ones? How do you plan to address these needs?
3. What is confusing about how your group or group members function? Can you give background?
4. Have there been specific problems related to loyalty, confidentiality, or availability?

APPENDIX F

Possible Themes for Continuing Education
For Peer Group Continuing Education

These themes assume that the thirteen chapters in *Called to Care* have been covered. You may want to return to study some themes in this book in greater depth. If so, add them to the list below.

Following are fifteen topics for possible study in continuing education. What concerns have you faced in your Care Group that are not listed? Nominate them for addition to the list. Then indicate the six you consider most important.

_____ 1. Feelings—Yours, Mine, and Ours
_____ 2. The Art of Listening
_____ 3. The Art of Leading Dialogue
_____ 4. Being Appropriately Assertive
_____ 5. Confidentiality
_____ 6. Utilizing Community Resources
_____ 7. Hospital Visitation
_____ 8. Ministering to Those Experiencing Grief
_____ 9. Ministering to the Dying
_____10. Ministering to Depressed Persons
_____11. Ministering to Suicidal Persons
_____12. Ministering to Older Persons
_____13. Ministering to Those Experiencing Divorce
_____14. Ministering to Inactive Members
_____15. Ministering to New Parents
_____16.
_____17.
_____18.
_____19.
_____20.

APPENDIX G

Training Program Evaluation Form
For those who have taken the training

Please fill out this form as it applies to your experience in the Care Group Leader Training Program. Thank you for helping us improve it. You need not sign your name.

1. How many sessions have you attended?

2. How would you rate the training program?
_____ Excellent _____ Good _____ Fair _____ Poor

3. What one thing do you feel is *most effective* in this training program and should be continued?

4. What one thing has been *least helpful* and could be discontinued?

5. What one thing was missing and might be added to make this training program *more effective?*

6. Comments about facilities, materials, instruction, etc., that might be helpful.

_____
Signature optional

Notes

1. John Mallison, *Building Small Groups in the Christian Community* (West Ryde, N.S.W. Australia: Renewal Publications, 1980), p. 11.

2. This vision is well outlined by Carl F. George in "A Small Group Strategy for the Church of the Future," an audio tape and seminar outline (Pasadena, Calif.: The Charles E. Fuller Institute of Evangelism and Church Growth, 1991).

3. Kenneth Haugk, *Christian Caregiving, A Way of Life* (Minneapolis, Minn.: Augsburg Publishing House, 1984).

4. Quoted by John Maxwell in *Small Groups Make a Big Difference* (Bonita, Calif.: Injoy Life Club, 1989).

5. Charles Colson, *Kingdoms in Conflict* (Grand Rapids, Mich.: Zondervan Publishers, 1987).

6. Adapted from Peter Wiwcharuck, *Building Effective Leadership* (Three Hills, Alberta: International Christian Leadership Development Foundation, Inc., 1987), p. 43.

7. Bruce Larson, *The Emerging Church* (Waco, Tex.: Word Books, 1970), chapter 2.

8. Dale Gallaway, *20/20 Vision* (Portland, Ore.: Scott Publishing Company, 1988).

9. Melvin J. Steinbron, *Can the Pastor Do it Alone?* (Ventura, Calif.: Regal Books, 1987).

10. For a more complete development of covenant content, see Louis Evans, Jr., *Covenant to Care* (Wheaton, Ill.: Victor Books, 1982).

11. Faith and Life Press, Box 347, Newton, KS 67114 (800 743-2484).

12. Serendipity House, Box 1012, Littleton, CO 80160 (800 525-9563).

13. Judy Hamlin, *The Curriculum and Small Group Resource Guide* (Colorado Springs, Colo.: Navpress, 1991).

14. Adapted from Roberta Hestenes, *Using the Bible in Groups* (Philadelphia, Pa.: Westminster Press, 1983), p. 22.

15. For more information on these groups, contact Linda Bos, Crystal Cathedral, 12141 Lewis, Garden Grove, CA 92640.

16. Order from Serendipity House.

17. Paul Miller, *Group Dynamics in Evangelism* (Scottdale, Pa.: Herald Press, 1958), p. 56.

18. Ibid., p. 84.

19. Ibid., p. 108.

20. Richard Peace, *Small Group Evangelism* (Downers Grove, Ill.: InterVarsity Press, 1985), p. 73.

21. Ibid., p. 73.

22. Ibid., p. 56.

23. You may want to sensitively use and expand an outline such as "Your Most Important Relationship," prepared by Youth For Christ, Box 419, Wheaton, IL 60189.

24. Judy Hamlin, *The Small Group Leaders Training Course* (Colorado Springs Colo.: Navpress, 1990), p. 100.

25. Paul Yonggi Cho, *Successful Home Cell Groups*, (South Plainfield, N.J.: Bridge Publishing, 1981).

26. Gordon Cosby, *Handbook to Mission Groups* (Waco: Word Books, Inc., 1975), p. 54.

27. Ibid., p. 59.

28. Kennon L. Callahan, *Twelve Keys to an Effective Church* (San Francisco: Harper & Row, 1983), p. 5.

29. For more information on these ministries, contact Jessica Moffett, First Methodist Church, 115 South Boulder, Tulsa, OK 74119.

30. Cosby, p. 60.

31. Ibid., p. 60.

32. Ibid., p. 62.

33. See especially Lyman Coleman, *Serendipity Youth Ministry Encyclopedia* (Littleton, Colo.: Serendipity House, 1985), p. 8.

34. For an excellent treatment on the use of sharing questions, see Hestenes, pp. 102-106.

35. Paul Tournier, *A Listening Ear* (Minneapolis: Fortress Books, 1986).

36. Staff member of Stephen Ministries, Saint Louis, Mo.

37. Wiwcharuck.

38. Hestenes, p. 106.

39. Appreciation is expressed to Mike Nichols, who introduced this concept of Bible study to group leaders at Peace Mennonite Church, Richmond, B.C., in 1982.

40. Alan Richardson, *Word Studies of the Bible* (New York: The Macmillan Company, 1950).

41. Published by Serendipity House.

42. Adapted from the classic by Rosalind Rinkers, *Prayer: Conversing with God* (Grand Rapids: Zondervan, 1959).

43. Steve Barker et al., *Small Group Leaders Handbook* (Downers Grove, Ill.: InterVarsity Press, 1982), pp. 173-175.

44. Judy Hamlin, *The Small Group Leaders Training Course* (Colorado Springs, Colo.: Navpress, 1990).

45. Callahan, p. 1.

46. Doug Whallon, *Good Things Come in Small Groups* (Downers Grove, Ill.: InterVarsity Press, 1985), p. 38.

47. John Maxwell, quoted from "Discipleship 89," Clearbrook, B.C.

48. George, p. 1.

49. Hestenes, pp. 40-42.

50. Albert J. Wollen, *How to Conduct Home Bible Classes* (Wheaton, Ill.: Scripture Press Publications, 1969), p. 19.

51. Coleman, p. 88.

52. Barker, p. 64.

53. Wiwcharuck, p. 268.

54. Coleman, p. 80.

55. Larson, p. 94.

56. Hamlin, p. 126.

57. Adapted from Roberta Hesteness, "Small Groups in the Church," a course outline, at Fuller Theological Seminary, Pasadena, Calif.

58. Miller, p. 98.

59. David W. Johnson and Frank P. Johnson, *Joining Together* (Englewood Cliffs, N.J.: Prentice-Hall, 1975), p. 229.

60. David Keirsey and Marilyn Bates, *Please Understand Me* (Del Mar, Calif.: Prometheus Nemesis Book Co., 1984).

61. David Augsburger, *Caring Enough to Confront* (Ventura, Calif.: Regal Books, 1980).

62. For a more complete treatment of this subject, see Kenneth Haugks excellent book, *Antagonists in the Church* (Minneapolis: Augsburg Publishing House, 1988).

The Author

Palmer Becker was born near Dolton, South Dakota, and raised on a dairy farm near Marion. He received his education from Freeman (S.D.) Junior College, Goshen (Ind.) College, Mennonite Biblical Seminary (Elkhart, Ind.), and Fuller Theological Seminary (Pasadena, Calif.). In his D.Min. program at Fuller, he outlined a new approach to catechism studies in "The Ministry of Membership Preparation."

Becker was a relief worker in Taiwan under the General Conference (GC) Mennonite Church in 1958-63. Seminary education and pastoring followed that. During the 1970s, Becker was called to lead the home mission and service ministries of the GC Mennonite Church. Under the banner of Living, Active Congregations, he promoted small groups and congregational outreach ministries throughout North America. During the 1980s, he was involved in church planting and university ministries in Vancouver (B.C.).

Becker is involved as a consultant and field trainer for the Living in Faithful Evangelism (LIFE) program for the Mennonite and Church of the Brethren denominations. He has pastored in Oklahoma, Kansas, British Columbia,

Minnesota, and Oregon, pioneering in developing small group ministries in each. He sees the small group as the key pastoral structure of the church.

He presently serves as Director of Pastoral Ministries at Hesston (Kansas) College and is the editor of "The Small Group Shepherd," a quarterly newsletter for small group leaders. His wife, Ardys, teaches Christian Education part-time at Hesston College and serves with Palmer in small-group ministries. The Beckers can be contacted for consultation by e-mail, palmerb@southwind.net, or by phone through the college, 1-316-327-4221.

Palmer and Ardys (Preheim) Becker are the parents of four grown children: Byron (Kitchener, Ont.), Jo (Suffern, N.Y.), Sharla (Kitchener, Ont.), and Steve (Coronado, Calif.). They also enjoy visiting their three grandchildren.